D0050366

# creative
# play
## for 2–5s

# creative play

Dr Dorothy Einon

## play
### for 2–5s

hamlyn

First published in Great Britain in 2005 by Hamlyn,
a division of Octopus Publishing Group Ltd
2–4 Heron Quays, London E14 4JP

Copyright © Octopus Publishing Group Ltd 2005

All rights reserved. No part of this work may be reproduced or
utilized in any form or by any means, electronic or mechanical,
including photocopying, recording or by any information
storage and retrieval system, without the prior written
permission of the publisher.

Distributed in the United States and Canada by
Sterling Publishing Co., Inc.
387 Park Avenue South, New York, NY 10016–8810

ISBN 0 600 61180 9
EAN 9780600611806

A CIP catalogue record for this book is available from the
British Library

Printed and bound in China

10 9 8 7 6 5 4 3 2 1

# Contents

# How to use this book

The desire to help a child to reach their full potential is at the forefront of most parents' minds. This book shows you how to provide a creative environment for your child and explains how your child's natural abilities can be supported and enhanced.

## Fulfilling potential

Most children are born with more potential than they will fulfil. Some do not try hard because they are afraid of failure, lack encouragement or believe they are not capable. Others have poor teachers or coaches, or lack the right tools or support. This book will tell you how to avoid some of these pitfalls and how best to raise a successful – but happy – child.

Helping your child achieve his full potential does not mean your aim is to make him a sports champion, a world-famous artist or a great actor. That sort of success takes an exceptional talent, an overriding ambition and a good deal of luck. It is not what this book is about. My aim is to show all parents how to help their children, whatever their abilities, to achieve their very best. The kind of well-rounded, successful children I have in mind will not necessarily win any of the races on sports day, make the football team, come top of the class or take the lead in the school play. They may do some of those things or they may do none of them. The aim is to help all children to use their full range of talents in every activity.

## Why foster creativity?

Gone are the days when a few years of schooling sufficed and skills, once learned, would last a lifetime. The world is changing at an increasing rate. Small children have the curiosity and confidence to try new things. They are not self-conscious or afraid to make mistakes. Creative people hang on to these skills throughout life. A child who is encouraged to be creative is likely to remain so and adapt to a changing world.

## Parents as teachers

Parents can be their child's best teachers. They know him better than anyone else, they can give one-to-one attention and choose the right moments to praise, to suggest solutions and offer constructive criticism. If he is restless they know the right moment to put on some music, so that he can dance around the room to let off steam and improve blood circulation to the brain before settling down to a more mentally demanding task. If a child is tired the parent can put away the activity and cuddle up with a book or in front of the television. However, parents can also expect too much, drive too hard, be over-critical or dismissive, which can damage their child's self-esteem. They can take over the child's motivation and take away all the pleasure he once took in an activity. They can also make a child feel stupid and incompetent, so that he becomes so sure he 'can't', that he never discovers that in fact he 'can'.

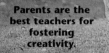

**Parents are the best teachers for fostering creativity.**

## How this book is structured

The first part of this book explains the nature of creativity and its links with imagination, intelligence and giftedness. It looks at the importance of the right environment and appropriate support in promoting a child's development, and how gender and the child's place within the family also play their part. Developmental charts enable you to see what the average child is capable of doing at various ages, while check lists help you recognize and develop his emerging talents by encouraging specific activities at the right level for your child. Later sections of the book focus on specific aspects of creativity. Throughout the book, there are practical suggestions for activities, toys and play equipment that will help your child develop and maximize his talents.

## Believing in your child

Your belief in your child's abilities is vital to his development. In the middle of the last century, a psychologist studied how 'labelling' a child could influence their ability in the eyes of a teacher. She conducted IQ tests, and told the teacher which children the tests suggested were the most intelligent and which were least intelligent. In fact, she had allocated children randomly to each group and there were no real differences between them. By the end of the year the children whom the teacher believed were bright were doing well and those she thought were less intelligent were doing badly. A cruel experiment for those labelled less intelligent – but one that is all too often repeated by parents and teachers who make premature assumptions that turn into self-fulfilling prophecies.

# What is creativity?

Creative people approach things in novel ways. It is not what they do, it is the way that they do it. It is possible to be a creative cook, a creative gardener and a creative thinker, just as it is possible to be an average but competent musician or artist.

Children will approach everyday activities in a naturally creative way.

### Children are naturally creative

Because the ability to plan activities and avoid distractions comes later, preschoolers are naturally creative. They do things first and think about them later, and they do them many times before they develop a set way of doing so – if indeed they ever do. While, as adults, we can say, 'I'll do A, then B, then C, D and E', young children usually think ahead no further than B. There is so much to learn in the early years, they cannot wait until they are mature enough to plan their learning strategy. They just have to get on with it.

### Children learn by doing

A child's inborn talents develop through experience. We can provide the right environment for those experiences but the child himself must make use of the opportunities offered. Nobody can learn for a child. We can coach, explain, praise, demonstrate and correct our children, but if their bodies and minds are not engaged, very little is learned. We can foster their engagement by always encouraging their curiosity and expecting them to try new things and experiences.

## Fostering creativity

• Remember that your child has an in-built plan that determines what needs to be learned and this will push him in the right direction. As he learns to control his fingers, you will see him pick up tiny objects; as his balance improves, you will see him run and jump. If you watch him with an open mind, you will start to learn where his talents lie and which activities need encouraging.

• Most children pass through the same stages at about the same time. Watch your child carefully and then look through this book to find an activity that is suitable. If he enjoys what he is doing you know that you have got it right.

• He does some things because they are necessary for his development and others because they get attention. It is usually easy to distinguish between the two, and once you have done this, you can focus on the activities that benefit him.

• It is important to encourage curiosity in your child, but sometimes you need to direct how questions are asked. Young children are more likely to ask questions in actions rather than words, which means we sometimes have to adapt the questions. If a toddler wants to know 'what happens if I pull that loose bit of wallpaper?' he pulls! And, if we allow it, he pulls again. To direct his curiosity in more acceptable ways without quashing it, we can, for example, stick a piece of masking tape to a door and let him pull that. Alternatively, we can provide more interesting and creative ways to ask 'What happens if I …?', such as encouraging him to play with water at the sink or with a bowl of rice or sand.

• He wants to please you and enjoys doing things that make you smile. At the same

A simple xylophone may encourage a child's interest in music.

time you want him to be happy and have fun. With a little thought, it is possible to provide opportunities for inventive and stimulating play that will fulfil both these needs. Take that perennially favourite game of throwing things out of his bed or highchair. Because throwing things makes him laugh, we pick up the toys. Because we smile and joke, he throws them out of the bed again. This means that he has plenty of practice at working out that the object that was once in his hand is the one that is now on the floor. This is an important step towards understanding that objects and people exist even when the child cannot touch or see them.

# Making connections

Some problems have only one solution and must be solved by convergent thinking; the sort of thinking that is measured by intelligence tests. Other types of problems encourage us to think of a variety of solutions. This sort of thinking is called divergent. It can lead us to solve problems in new and creative ways.

## Intelligence and creativity

Standard intelligence tests, such as the IQ (intelligence quotient) test, measure convergent thinking. They are based on questions that have right and wrong answers. Because this sort of thinking is required for a high proportion of schoolwork, those who achieve high scores in intelligence tests also tend to do well in school exams.

By contrast, when we try to measure creativity, we ask questions that have lots of possible answers and that encourage divergent ways of thinking. A question on an IQ test might be 'What is the next letter in the sequence JFMAMJ?' (The answer is J – the letters represent the initial letters of the months of the year.) A question in a creativity test might be 'What would happen if everyone suddenly went blind?' It is clear that some people could score more highly in one test than in the other – that is, not all intelligent people are creative or vice versa.

## Do IQ tests really measure intelligence?

Whole books have been written on this topic. The consensus view is 'not exactly'. Because of the way the questions are worded, IQ tests favour middle-class children who are members of the dominant culture. This means that the results of children of different ethnic and class origins cannot be compared. Within any ethnic group, however, IQ test scores are a good predictor of academic success and achievement. So, while we can argue about what an IQ score means, it is hard to dispute that some people are more intelligent than others.

Just because someone is bright and does well at school it does not mean that they do not have blind spots or are necessarily good at reading people's intentions or are self-aware in ways that might be called smart. One thing that is certain is that the sort of thinking IQ tests measure is not the sort that preschoolers use.

## How young children think

Convergent thinking is logical, so until children can think logically (at about the age of seven) they are not convergent thinkers. Neither are they divergent thinkers. They are linear thinkers – that is, they latch on to the solution that strikes them first, which is usually the one that looks right. For example, a young child may think there is more clay in a ball than when the same clay is rolled out into a sausage, because the ball is higher. Or, when he sees the water being sucked down the drain in the bath, he may start to believe that he will be sucked down as well.

When a young child is asked what he is drawing, he may tell you it is a house; but the following day he may think it looks more like a car and will tell you this is what he drew. It is this tendency to change their minds over time that makes us think of young children as creative thinkers.

## What is talent?

Talent is much more specific than creativity. Artistic talent rarely spills over into music and a talent for golf may not even extend to other ball games. Talent gives the possibility of lifting achievement in a particular field beyond the technically competent. However, it needs a bedrock of competence. This is not to say that every child has the same potential for gaining technical competence. Outside his special area of expertise, a talented person is often no more creative than others.

## Imagination

A child's first communication is usually an action. His arms go up to say 'pick me up', and when he vocalizes his first words there is usually an action and a word. For example, the way he says 'look at the cat' is to point and say 'pss'. We can think of his imaginative play as like those actions; a way of thinking things through in movement and images rather than words. But it goes further than this. As he grows up, his increasingly complex games of pretence become his way of story-telling and exercising his vivid imagination. The more elaborate the pretence, the more likely he is to have a vivid imagination.

If your child likes to dance and shows talent, encourage her as much as you can.

## Insight from research

Studies of the achievements of precocious children, who have later gone on to become, for example, pioneers of scientific research, top athletes, inventors or musicians, all reveal that the children had extensive training from talented teachers and exceptionally dedicated parental support.

# Encouraging natural talents

We can never say where an individual's particular talents come from. We know that genes, upbringing, training, personality and experience all play a role but not how much each contributes. Neither do we expect the formula to be the same for each individual.

## Genes

Genetic endowment ensures that children are likely to have brains, bodies and possibly talents that are like those of their parents. In as far as your build is that of a long-distance runner or a weight-lifter, your child is likely to be built in the same way. If you have good mathematical skills, your child is likely to inherit that potential. Yet, because we also inherit a culture and a way of parenting, the environment that nurtured our skills is also likely to nurture those of our children and, sadly, those environments that stifled our creativity can be recreated for our children.

## Environment

The environment also plays a vital role in a child's development. For instance, fifty years ago only 10 per cent of British children obtained any exam passes at the age of 15, and many of those got passes in only one or two subjects. Today even schools that perform badly in league tables get better results than this. The exams have not got easier; the pupils have grown brighter. We know this because children have been taking the same IQ tests since the First World War. Every couple of years the average IQ goes up a point. So a child considered exceptional in 1914 would be considered quite ordinary today.

## Establishing a creative environment

It is not the toys, the books or the physical environment that are most important. It is the child's social environment that really counts. Money cannot buy love and giving limited amounts of quality time is no substitute for total involvement. You could fill the house with toys and his waking hours with activity without really adding much of value to your child's development.

Everything a small child learns he learns first within a social context. The way caregivers interact with children on a day-to-day and minute-to-minute basis makes the real difference. Experts call this constructive creativity. This is more about family dynamics and self-esteem than the expensive mobile over the bed.

## Creativity is likely to be fostered when:
• Children are encouraged to feel free to express their feelings or opinions. Families are open to new experiences and different opinions.

• Children are encouraged to manipulate and evaluate ideas. For example, when parents seek their child's opinion and lead them forward with questions such as 'Why do you think that …?' and 'What would happen if …?'
• Children are allowed to be creative and original and as they grow up they are encouraged to consider more than one solution to each problem.
• Discipline is firm without being punitive and with clear limits so that children are able to become self-disciplined. There is no point in having 50 ideas an hour if you never follow any of them through.

**Provide the materials to stimulate your child's creativity.**

• Parents have confidence their child will behave well and do their best.
• Parents accept or tolerate their child's creative ideas without being dismissive or belittling achievements.
• Parents support their child when she risks being different.
• Parents have confidence in their child's ability. Do not say 'That's too hard' before she has tried. If it proves to be too hard, tell her you are proud that she made the attempt at all.
• Parents are prepared to let their child pursue an activity when she is obviously enjoying herself.
• Parents provide direction in finding problems as well as solving them. The key question is 'Why do you think that …?'.
• Parents allow free expression alongside specific training and plenty of opportunity for practice. Remember even great artists had drawing lessons.
• Parents are creative themselves. Children copy what we do.
• Children have contact with other creative thinkers through books, TV and discussions with adults and older children.
• Conformity is replaced by an openness. Decide which values are important in your family and be flexible on the rest.
• Parents encourage make-believe and imaginative play.
• Children are exposed to stories, art and music, as well as ideas and physical activities, including dance and sports.

# Birth order

Take any list of great achievers, whether they are writers, scientists or business executives, and you will find that eldest children are the most successful. In modern times, this appears to be equally true of sons and daughters.

## First-borns

There are only adults in a first-born's family and so he sees himself as an extension of the adult world. When brothers and sisters come along, he also becomes one of the 'children'. The average first-born tends to be socially more mature and more self-controlled for his age than his younger siblings. The first-born may take on the role of manager, helper and teacher to the younger children.

Parents have higher expectations of their first-born and he needs their approval more than his siblings do. This is why some first-borns are insecure and afraid of letting people down. First-borns tend to do better at school, however, even if they are no cleverer than their younger brothers and sisters. Some first-borns are overprotected and overindulged, while others may receive rather harsher treatment than their younger siblings.

## Later children

Subsequent children are born into a family that is already child-oriented, and from the start they see themselves as 'one of the children'. They watch and imitate their older brothers and sisters. They are more likely to seek friendship outside the family, to be extroverted and pleasure-seeking. Second children tend to be less conventional and they do less well in IQ tests and at school. One suggestion is that middle children are more likely to have creative ideas.

## Youngest children

By the time the last child is born parents are often more relaxed. Youngest children are more likely to be indulged by parents and older siblings. They tend to have all the drive to succeed that their eldest siblings have, but because the family is settled they have none of the insecurity and doubt that can plague the eldest child.

## Do not label

Studies indicate that it may be the parent's expectations of their first, middle and youngest child that has the most lasting influence on the child's development. Whether this is true or not, parents should compensate for birth-order effects. When individual needs are different and a parent's attention is limited, someone has to be first in the queue and someone has to be last. Every child should have a time each day when they are first, but should also take their turn at the back.

# The role of gender

Over the past 50 years, the roles of men and women have become much less distinct. Yet the gender identity (the sense of being either a woman or a man) is just as clear for most people today as it has always been.

## Roles and identity

As soon as she can say the right word, a child will tell you her gender. By age four, she is pretty fixed on the idea that girls grow up to be women, but she is closer to seven before she is certain that her gender cannot be altered.

Children learn about sex roles from the people they see about them – from their family, their friends, the media and books. They start by seeing men's and women's roles as defined by the things we segregate (like going fishing or making dresses). However, by age seven or eight, their views are more likely to reflect behaviour within their own family.

Differences between the sexes do not become apparent until a child is seven or eight.

## Learning gender identity

Gender identity is distinct from the sex roles you adopt or your sexual preferences. It is central to your feeling of self. No sensible parent has a liberal attitude towards their child's gender identity – children who are uncertain whether they are a boy or a girl are likely to be very unhappy.

In past generations it was easy to see what gender roles were, but today it is much harder. For young children the essence of woman seems to be embodied in a fashion doll, and that of man in a macho boy's toy, possibly indicating that today's children are in need of simple stereotypes.

## How do boys and girls differ?

Boys are more vulnerable: they are more likely to be accident prone, to have serious illnesses and to have speech and behaviour problems. We tend to think of boys as more aggressive, noisy and boisterous, and of girls as quieter and more organized.

The younger children are, especially boys, the harder it is for them to settle down. On average, boys reach puberty two years later than girls; girls crawl, walk and talk earlier than boys. When school starts, most boys are not ready to spend as much of the day sitting as girls.

# Boosting confidence through creativity

Children with high self-esteem tend to be less conformist and more creative, and highly creative children usually have a high level of self-esteem. By encouraging and supporting our children's creativity, we not only make them feel better about themselves but also improve their chances of success.

## Self-esteem

By the age of two, children have an idea of their age, gender and position in the family. They recognize themselves in pictures and in the mirror. They see themselves as good or bad, clever or stupid, without making any finer distinctions. They do not understand that you can be clever at some things and not others.

Two-year-olds focus on the present: today he is the little boy in the red shorts who likes to paddle; tomorrow he will be the boy in the blue jumper who falls off his bike. Self-esteem varies from situation to situation. If a child thinks he is good at drawing, his self-esteem goes up when he draws. If he thinks he is bad at singing, it goes down when he sings. As a child grows up, this situation-specific self-esteem is reinforced or moderated by background self-esteem, which is fed by all his perceived competencies and failures.

## What influences esteem?

Children with high self-esteem tend to have parents with high self-esteem. They are more likely to have a good and secure attachment to their caregivers and to be treated firmly, fairly and consistently by them. Against this background, the boosting of confidence or its deflation is affected by whatever is important to the child. Success inflates self-esteem and failure deflates it. Because high self-esteem makes it easier to succeed, success builds success and, conversely, failure breeds failure.

## How to build self-esteem

• Love him for himself, not what he can do.
• Criticize the behaviour, never your child. He is a special boy, who has on this occasion behaved in a bad way.
• Take care to pitch activities so that your child is drawn forward gradually.
• Show him you are proud that he has tried his best, whether or not he has succeeded in the activity.
• Provide your child with challenges so that he can experience the boost to self-esteem that succeeding in something difficult brings.
• Choose challenges for your child that carry a minimum risk of failure. If he constantly fails, his self-esteem will plummet.
• Do not build up the importance of success before he has attempted the activity. If he succeeds at an activity, give generous praise afterwards.

# Creativity for special children

Children with special needs may not be able to supply their own motivation for their own actions, or be able to see or hear the objects or events that would normally draw children into an activity. They may, therefore, need extra encouragement.

## Different problems

Although special children all need encouragement and support, their specific needs vary. A child with learning difficulties may have trouble motivating herself for activity and creativity; a child with physical disabilities may have problems making fine movements or handling small objects. Society is likely to underestimate the capabilities of a child with special needs, and this can undermine the child's self-esteem.

## Encouraging development

A child with special needs develops along the same path as other children, just at a different speed and a different time. She needs the same tools and activities, but they may need to be adapted. For example, if she finds it difficult to move, a sloping surface will ensure that toys slide back into her lap.

Fifty years ago no one would have believed you could play tennis in a wheelchair, let alone play it well. The easiest way to avoid your child's disability becoming her defining characteristic is to make sure she joins in any activity that interests her.

## Building confidence

• Let her try – however long it takes.
• Do not be overprotective. She has to learn to fight her own battles.
• Let her know just how special she is to you by showing your love and appreciation at all times.
• Expect success. Do not let disability become an excuse for you or your child.
• If her fine finger control is poor, give her a big crayon or a large brush.

Even if children have significant co-ordination problems, they will still enjoy producing a painting and having fun.

# Order and method

When your child first opens the piano and bangs the keys, she is just pretending to play. To be a creative musician, however, she has to understand the language of music and to have the practical skills to play an instrument or sing in tune.

## Symbols and emotions

The ability to use symbols opens the doors to countless creative experiences. Objects and actions are sometimes symbols; words and pictures are rarely anything else. The first words most children learn are those that describe familiar objects and creatures. Only later do they talk about or act out their feelings. When your child sings, you know she is happy. When all the people she draws have knees, she may be depicting a fall she had when she grazed her knee. She is expressing herself spontaneously and openly.

## Developing artistic skills

To become a creative artist, however, a child must develop the technical skills to play music, dance, act, tell stories or draw pictures. Children need teachers to provide constructive criticism and help them approach their chosen activity in a methodical and organized way.

## Keeping the balance

Most young children are naturally expressive, but structure and method require formal practice. As well as free drawing, a child needs to learn how to use a pencil or a brush with precision. As well as telling you things in an excited jumble, a child needs to express herself clearly. At first it is easiest to separate the two types of expression, but in time she will naturally bring these skills together.

## Avoiding burnout

If you push a child too hard, you will run the risk of burnout. If a family plays musical instruments, a child is likely to want to join in; but wanting to play is different from wanting to practise an instrument every night. Surveys suggest that many musical children give up because they started to play too young. Problems arise for those who are pushed into it and find it difficult. Follow these simple guidelines:

• Do not start formal lessons – whether music, dancing or reading – too soon.
• No one can be creative for someone else. It must come from his heart, not yours.
• Demonstrate creativity rather than impose it.
• Creativity needs freedom and structure. Allow your child to experience both.
• Do not appropriate your child's creative pursuits. You have to live your own life, just as your children have to live theirs.
• Always show your child that you love him for himself alone and not for what he can do.
• Praise his effort regardless of his success or achievement.

# Possible problems

There is no reason why a creative child should have more problems at home or school than his less-creative sibling. Neither is it more likely that a troubled child will be more creative than one who is socially well adapted.

## Emotional openness

At first, all children freely express emotion – crying when they are sad, laughing when they are happy. In time, some are taught to 'button up', while others continue to express their emotions more freely. The simple message for all those wishing to raise creative children is that there is nothing wrong with having feelings and showing them. Let them know this.

## Feeling and acting

A creative child needs the same emotional support as any other child, and his creativity should not be used to excuse inappropriate behaviour or to blind us to possible problems that really need to be addressed. Do not let your creative child manipulate the family by threats of emotional outbursts. Such behaviour will not endear him to teachers or other children. Teaching your child to express his emotions in an appropriate way will not impede his creativity.

Very few children have tantrums with people they do not know and love, nor do they rush up and cuddle them. If he is very promiscuous with his emotions, this is not a sign of artistic promise, but more likely to be a sign of impending problems. Some children are naturally more solitary than others, but being a loner is not always what a child chooses for himself. If it is not his choice, he will be unhappy. Help him to find a like-minded friend. Talk to his teachers and do not dismiss their views. They know how your child acts in the company of strangers.

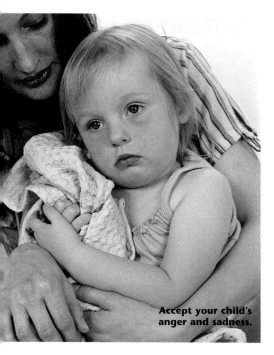
**Accept your child's anger and sadness.**

# Development 2–2½ years of age

Children develop at different rates. A child who is advanced in whole-body motor skills will probably have good hand-eye co-ordination, but having better than average motor skills does not predict how advanced language, social and learning skills will be. Nor do these skills advance together. Remember, children do not grow or grow up at a smooth rate. He will sometimes seem to stand still and at other times leap ahead.

## Whole-body movement

• He can walk and talk, and walk and pull along or carry a toy.
• He can sit on his bike and scoot with his feet.
• He runs with flat feet and short strides but good co-ordination, but is not able to stop or control his speed very well. He cannot easily change direction on the run.
• He does not need to use the buggy for short trips.
• He can briefly stand on tiptoes.
• He holds the rail to climb stairs. Leads with one foot, resting both feet on the same step between strides.
• He can jump a short distance off the ground and hop on one foot. Makes lots of arm movements but does not crouch.
• He moves his bike (and himself) around an obstacle.

## Hand–eye co-ordination

• He prefers to use either his left or right hand.
• He uses pincer grip and power grip to pick up and hold objects. (That is, uses his thumb in opposition to his finger(s).) He can point, prod, stroke, twist and turn. He can place and drop toys.
• He can put one brick on top of another and may be able to use a simple construction kit. He can put pieces in a puzzle tray.
• He looks at books, and is able to point to the images.
• He threads big beads on to a string.
• He can do up large buttons.
• He can control a crayon and may be able to copy a line you have drawn for him.
• He can use a spoon and may start to use a fork.

## Language

• He knows 50 words at two, several hundred words by two and a half.
• He uses two-word sentences, increasing to three words.
• He starts to use pronouns (me, she) and prepositions (in, on) but his language is still rather telegraphic, with short sentences and some missing words and word endings.
• He talks about activities if encouraged, can tell you what he wants, and understands simple instructions.
• He loves having books read to him and remembers simple stories.
• He likes to see your face when you speak to him.
• He knows his name and perhaps where he lives.
• He expresses recurrence 'more ball'; nonexistence 'all gone milk'; attribution 'big ball'; nomination 'that ball'; agent action 'Frankie hit'; and agent action object 'Frankie hit ball'.
• His words are clearer.

## Social skills

• He is affectionate and loving.
• He tends to be clingy in strange places or with strange people.
• He has tantrums but only with those people he loves. Tantrums are unpredictable. Once over, it is as if nothing has happened and he will return to his normal self.
• He begins to share, but may snatch back toys that belong to him.
• He enjoys being with other children.
• He knows he is a boy.
• He can feed himself – although still messy. He begins to dress himself – but needs help and makes mistakes such as getting shoes on the wrong feet.
• He insists on trying to do things for himself but is not realistic about his capabilities. He gets upset when he fails.
• He starts to play with other children but may snatch toys and can be quite rough.

## Learning

• He investigates why things happen and repeats these investigations over and over again. He watches and becomes engrossed in activities.
• He identifies himself in photographs, recognizes himself in the mirror.
• He imitates and plays simple pretend games. He ascribes human properties to animals and objects.
• He remembers simple rhymes and songs and joins in actions. Knows if you turn over two pages in a favourite book.
• He loves outings and new experiences.
• He can divide toys into simple categories (such as teddies and cars), but he cannot sort out cars into finer groups (such as big and small cars). He can match two bricks of the same colour.
• He understands that money buys things – but has no sense of the value of money.

# Development
# 2½–3 years of age

Although children develop in leaps and bounds, they do not always catch up with children who reached earlier milestones ahead of them. A child who is a little late reaching one set of milestones will be a little late in reaching the next, but eventually she will reach the same level. If there are longer developmental delays, problems are more likely to persist. Always have a developmental check if you are worried.

## Whole-body movement

• She enjoys walking along a log or wall if you hold her hand.
• She can stand on one foot and balance for several seconds at a time.
• She goes up stairs bringing feet together but alternating the starting foot. She walks down stairs leading with the same foot.
• She can climb ladders and use slides.
• She can jump from the bottom step of the stairs without losing her balance.
• She can copy the movements of an action song.
• She may insist on walking even when you prefer to use the buggy.
• She can easily walk on tiptoe without over-balancing.
• She can use the pedals of her bike – but may still prefer to scoot.
• She runs fast with confidence, but is still flat-footed, and cannot control her direction, speed or stopping very well.

## Hand–eye co-ordination

• She starts to draw circles, enclosures and crosses.
• She enjoys clay, sand and water and will like to squeeze a sponge and pour from a jug.
• She can do simple tray puzzles and make simple constructions.
• She can snip paper but cannot cut around things.
• She can carry out and enjoy simple household tasks such as dusting a table.
• She looks at books, points to images.
• She can control a crayon and may be able to copy simple shapes.
• She can dress herself, but still makes mistakes and cannot manage zippers and small buttons. She makes less mess when she feeds herself.

## Language

• She learns about 50 new words every month and will know about 1,000 words by age three. Speaks in two- or three-word sentences. Language is still quite telegraphic but is becoming clearer.
• She can tell you the names of her family and pets and where she lives.
• She uses 'in' and 'on'.
• She uses pronouns 'I', 'me' and 'my' frequently, but not always correctly.
• She issues instructions. May use words to express how she feels.
• She likes stories with her picture books.
• She can now follow more complex language and idioms.
• She says 'I walking', 'I doing'.
• She asks what words mean and what objects are called.
• She adds the 's' to words to make the plural (two balls) and to denote possession (Frankie's ball), and can use past tense 'Chair broke' and verb inflections 'He walks'.

## Social skills

• She is affectionate and loving, may comfort a child who is crying.
• She may still cling but is happy to be left at playschool. In a familiar place, she will go and play with other children.
• She has fewer tantrums. Tantrums are often more predictable and last for longer. She may be in a 'mood' before the tantrum and sometimes seems to induce them on purpose by asking for things that she knows she cannot have or which she knows she cannot do. She is often sad and sorry after the tantrum is over.
• She has a distinct sense of self and is protective of her possessions. She shares at playschool but may not do so at home.
• She likes to choose what to eat and wear.
• She likes being with other children and copes better in a crowd. She may form a friendship with another child, but it is likely to be fleeting.
• She may insist on trying to do things for herself but is not always realistic about her capabilities. She gets upset when she fails.
• She is more amenable to family rules.

## Learning

• She gossips and can make up simple stories.
• She can remember what happened yesterday. She can remember exciting events from the more distant past. Situations elicit memories. She remembers when she gets to the park what happened when she was last there, but will not have mentioned this before.
• She repeats things to help herself to remember them.
• She completes jigsaws with three or four large pieces.
• She can compare the size or height of two objects and comment on the difference (but not always correctly).

# Development 3–3½ years of age

By three, children are much more like their adult selves than their baby selves. Many of the characteristics that will define him as an adult are now present in embryonic form. Studies suggest that shy and withdrawn three-year-olds tend to grow up to be rather shy and withdrawn adults. If children are very aggressive and difficult at this age, they are also more likely to be difficult and antisocial adults.

## Whole-body movement

• Running is more fluid, but still flat-footed. He cannot turn or stop quickly.
• He can jump 5–10 times on both feet and hop 2–5 times on one foot. He uses lots of arm movements. He jumps with a small crouch, but does not bend knees to land.
• He jumps off a step.
• He can hurdle a jump about 7.5–10cm (3–4 inches).
• He goes up and down stairs and ladders one foot at a time.
• He walks on a wall leading with one foot, drawing the other foot forward to meet it.
• He can walk on a 7.5cm (3 inches) beam forwards 2m (6 feet) and backwards about 1m (3 feet).
• He will enjoy walking on walls and tree trunks, and may be able to do this without holding on.
• He skips with one foot and then walks the second foot to meet it.

## Hand–eye co-ordination

• He places things with greater care and precision and puts pieces into his jigsaw with less force.
• Construction skills improve.
• He can complete a jigsaw with about eight pieces – even more if he is given lots of practice.
• He can build a tower of eight or possibly more pieces.
• He enjoys water and sand play. He pours accurately.
• Tool use improves. He can feed himself without making too much mess, can use scissors to snip and copy a simple shape you have drawn.
• He can set the table and dust a shelf.
• He is increasingly skilful at dressing himself. He can wash his face with a cloth and use a toothbrush.

## Language

- He uses 'wh' questions a lot – where, why, what?
- He knows about 800–1,000 words at three years of age and adds about 50 new words a month.
- He uses two- to four-word sentences, and will string these together. Will tell you what he wants and how he feels. He can tell you about his day.
- He asks questions using 'can', 'have' and 'did'. The word order may not be right.
- He uses negative – 'I don't like cabbage', 'This isn't my coat' and 'I didn't do it'.
- He says 'I am walking' and 'I do like you' using the auxiliary verbs.

## Social skills

- He is able to play without checking you are there.
- He talks about what he does. Boasts.
- Tantrums are less frequent but more predictable. He is likely to be moody beforehand and sad and sorry afterwards. He needs comforting.
- He is more amenable to family rules.
- He has a distinct sense of self and is protective of his possessions.
- He likes to choose his own clothes, food and activities.
- He begins to choose activities because certain children are playing.
- He enjoys playing interactive games with other children.
- He socializes and plays with unfamiliar adults – even when the main caregiver is not around.

- He copies what other children and adults say and do.
- Sex role stereotypes are deeply ingrained into his view of the world.

## Learning

- He talks as if you share his experiences and can see everything he sees.
- He can do jigsaws and puzzles of four or more pieces.
- He can sort things into categories on the basis of one attribute (white and coloured washing) and match things one to one.
- He draws enclosed spaces, lines, shapes and crosses.
- He believes death is transient. He may think bad things happen because he is naughty. He believes that, if A causes B, then B also causes A, so that, if he bumps into the chair, the chair bumped into him.
- Understanding of causality depends on how close one thing is to another. So, for example, the engine noise might be what makes the car go.

# Development 3½–4 years of age

By three and a half, the last shreds of babyhood have been cast aside, and suddenly he is a toddler no more. Not yet self-conscious, but communicative, open and loving, it is a magical age. By four, he can move much as an adult moves, can talk much as an adult talks, and is beginning to understand what it is to be moral and responsible for his actions.

## Whole-body movement

• He is beginning to control starts, stops and turns as he runs, and his stride length is increasing, though he is still flat-footed.
• He can jump ten times on both feet and hop five times. He will try to gallop but will probably not succeed. Jumps and hops still look stiff. Not much spring in his jumps but with lots of arm movements. He starts with a minimal crouch on take-off and lands from the jump without bending his knees.
• He can jump down about 80cm (30 inches). He enjoys trampolines or jumping on the bed.
• He will start to ascend stairs using alternate feet, but will still go down one foot at a time.
• He may be able to put his knee on the ground from a standing position and rise again without touching the floor.
• He can walk on a 7.5cm (3 inch) beam forwards 2.5m (7½ feet) and backwards 1.5m (4 feet).

• He skips with one foot and then walks the second foot to meet it.
• He can start to copy the movements you show him.

## Hand–eye co-ordination

• The simplest figures emerge in his paintings and drawings.
• He is able to dress himself, although he may still get shoes on the wrong feet and have problems with zippers and buttons.
• He lines up jigsaw puzzle pieces before putting them in, and may be able to connect to two or three other pieces at a time.
• He can use Lego to build and put together simple toy kits.
• He eats and drinks without dropping food on clothes or getting it all over his hands and face.
• He rolls clay into a ball and cuts it with a blunt knife.
• His movements are smooth and efficient.

## Language
• He knows about 1,250 words at three and a half, and learns about 50 new words every month.
• He uses three- or four-word sentences that have a more complex structure – 'You think I can do it', 'I see what you mean'. He will be able to tell you a simple story.
• He has difficulty answering why, where and what questions (but he asks them).
• He uses 'if' and 'because'.

## Social skills
• He plays well with other children, but is still very possessive about his own toys. He is more likely to play with children of his own sex, but groups are still often mixed.
• He may have a special friend and chooses activities because children he likes are playing.
• He plays 'social' pretend games with two or three other children.
• He boasts less. Being liked becomes more important but he can still play alone in a crowded room.
• Children reinforce appropriate sex role behaviour and beliefs.

## Learning
• He enjoys constructing things, but may not plan ahead, so towers topple and things do not fit together as originally planned. He gets very frustrated when things go wrong.
• He will still talk as if you share his experiences and see what he sees (even though you are facing him).
• His first figures are drawn with irregular-shaped heads. Eyes may be placed near the edge of the head or together in the top left of the face.
• He gossips and talks about the past and future. He explains why he thinks something happened.

# Development 4–4½ years of age

By four, your child is beginning to move out into the world. She may still tell you what she has been doing, but you probably need to ask. By this age, most children are spending some part of the day away from their families and with other children. It is hard to pinpoint quite why she seems more grown up, but she does.

## Whole-body movement
• She runs with much more control over when she starts, stops and turns, but is still rather flat-footed and cannot dodge well. She begins to lift off the ground between steps as she runs.
• She will try to gallop, but probably will not succeed.
• She may be able to do about seven hops but without much spring and she still moves her arms rather a lot.
• She goes up stairs using an alternate foot pattern, but comes down one foot at a time.
• She can walk on a 7.5cm (3 inch) beam forwards 2.5m (7½ feet) and backwards 2m (6 feet).
• She can do a standing jump of 20cm (8 inches), a running jump of 60cm (24 inches) and a hurdle jump of 23cm (9 inches).

## Hand–eye co-ordination
• She draws human figures with faces, eyes and noses. They may have legs but probably not bodies. She draws simple houses and buildings and may begin to draw crude boats and cars.
• She may be able to do puzzles with 10–25 pieces if she is given lots of practice and encouragement.
• She can dress herself in all but the most difficult items.
• She can use a fork and spread butter with a knife.
• She can throw a small ball and catch a large one. She uses arms and hands to hold the ball as she catches.
• She can cut with scissors, but still has difficulty cutting out.

## Language

• She knows about 1,800 words and learns about 50 new words per month.
• She uses four- and five-word sentences.
• She uses conjunctions: 'You think I can but I can't'.
• She will tell her soft toys a story and pretend to read them a book. She talks through her actions as she plays and may say what she is doing.
• She will understand, but probably not produce, sentences such as 'He knew that John would win the race'.

## Social skills

• She plays well with other children and may choose an activity to be with a friend, but she is not unhappy when she is playing alone.
• She laughs and talks with other children. She begins to be able to take on roles in shared play.
• She prefers to play with children of her own gender. Her view of the difference between the sexes is stereotyped and is influenced by her peers.
• She knows that she will grow up to be a woman (and that he will grow up to be a man) but still believes that if a boy wears a dress he could become a woman.

## Learning

• Children take the perspective of another and relate it to their own. So she will explain to you who the child was that she played with at school, instead of assuming that you know.
• She can put together two or more ideas and form a conclusion.
• She can eat without making a mess.
• She can set the table and sort things into two different groups, but still has difficulty putting things in order.
• She may be able to recognize letters and numbers and may be able to write her name.

# Development 4½–5 years of age

Your child now moves more like a little adult than a baby, and being a little adult also characterizes many of her other skills and attributes. There is a sense in which you feel she is a young, immature version of what she will later become. Outgoing or shy, serious or light-hearted, emotional or self-contained – which is right? She now has a great deal more in common with herself at 16 years than herself at 16 months.

## Whole-body movement

• She takes longer strides. She can run 35 metres (yards) in 20–30 seconds.
• She gallops, but it is rather like a run and leap.
• She may hop about nine times.
• She goes up stairs and ladders using alternate feet. She uses alternate feet to come down the stairs but leads with one foot when coming down a ladder.
• She can walk about 3m (8–10 feet) forwards on a 7.5cm (3 inch) balance beam and about 2m (5–7 feet) backwards.
• She can do a standing jump of 25cm (10 inches), a running jump of 83cm (33 inches) and a hurdle jump of 23cm (9 inches).

## Hand–eye co-ordination

• She draws people with faces, legs and possibly arms.
• She can use small brick construction kits and follow simple building instructions, but will need advice and help.
• She may be able to form most letters. She colours outline drawings, but not very neatly.
• She throws a small ball more accurately; she may use an over-arm throw, but cannot aim very well. Her catching improves, but she still needs the ball to be thrown to her. She still gathers the ball into her body and cannot manage a small ball.
• She can put soap on a cloth and toothpaste on a toothbrush and will wash her face and brush her teeth. She can dry her hands and face, but does not dry her body.

## Language
• She knows about 1,500 words and learns about 50 new words per month.
• She uses four- and five-word sentences that she strings together.
• She will tell her soft toys a story and pretend to read them a book. She talks through her actions as she plays, and may say what she is doing as she does it.
• She uses conjunctions: 'You think I can but I can't'; 'Jenny and I are playing'.

## Social skills
• She understands that people do not share her thoughts and feelings.
• She chooses activities to be with friends.
• She may have a best friend. She will be upset if they fall out.
• She enjoys gossiping and will gossip with two or three people.
• She plays in bigger groups, but still finds it easier to talk and play one to one or one to two.

## Learning
• She can play simple board games, but does not use strategy.
• She remembers where things have been left, and does well in games that challenge this ability.
• She can match one to one and can count. She understands three is more than two but may not understand that six is more than five.
• She dresses herself, puts on her coat and shoes, but will still need help with laces and zippers. She eats neatly and can use a knife to cut, but will need help cutting up meat.
• She can do more complex constructions, jigsaw puzzles with more pieces and construction kits with smaller pieces. She begins to plan ahead.
• She co-ordinates two or more ideas into a single skill.
• Her figures have limbs and she may add hair and fingers. She draws houses and cars.
• She will tell jokes, but does not understand why they are funny.

# art and craft

# Learning to draw

Children start to put marks on paper as soon as they are able to hold a crayon. This activity reinforces a child's awareness that he can make things happen. If you display the drawings, your child will know they are special.

First faces often occur in children's drawings as a matter of chance.

As pictures become more advanced, so do the details.

A sense of proportion and scale will develop over time.

## First drawings

A child starts to draw by making big swirls without taking the crayon off the paper. Later he starts to lift the crayon from time to time and can produce lines and dots. By the age of three and a half, he will be able to produce circles, squares, dots, big swirls and little squiggles. He is starting to do more than scribble; he now realizes that drawings represent things. His first 'face' is probably a matter of chance. A circle and a dot happen to look like a face so he adds a second eye. We are delighted and tell him he is a clever boy, so he does it again, gradually refining the face. The head is probably oddly shaped and the features may not be in the right place, but they are there.

## His world in pictures

As he starts to draw intentionally, his pen control improves, his heads are round and the eyes are put in the right place. He starts to add legs to the face. He may draw lots of legs at first, but eventually he settles on two legs that come out at the bottom of the head. He may add arms to the head or draw a separate body. Whichever he does, the arms will be attached about halfway down. Next he adds a varying number of fingers and some hair.

Nothing is drawn to scale; the more important a feature is, the bigger he draws it. The subject of his drawings varies to reflect important events in his life – for example, if he has a sore throat, his people may have necks. He draws what should be there, not what he sees. Faces always look out of the page, animals stand side on with their faces turned to the viewer. Dogs have four legs and a tail, and cats have whiskers.

## Form and composition

By the age of four his pictures are taking shape. His faces used to emerge from the scribble; now they stand alone on the page. There is a sense of balance in the way he arranges the elements on the paper. The main character probably stands just off centre and there is usually an equal amount of embellishment on either side. At first he adds this embellishment to the basic figure, but gradually he includes extra features to cover the page. He may draw grass and flowers on each side of the house, a sun shining on one side of the figure and birds flying on the other.

Yet, although by five he makes a composition, his drawings are a collection of separate parts. The car hovers above the road, the man floats above the stool (which has a seat and all four legs in view), chimneys are perpendicular to the roof, and houses perpendicular to the hill rather than the page so they cling at an angle.

Flowers must have petals and, like the faces of animals and people, are seen from the front. Trees look like lollipops with brown straight trunks and round green tops. People's feet are seen in profile. When he draws his family, he will be as big as, or bigger than, his parents. Even if he lives in an apartment or a semi-detached house, he will draw a detached house. He will not start to draw what he really sees until he is seven or eight years old.

# Talent spotter

★ **Does your child draw without encouragement?**

★ **Even when she scribbled, was the drawing well placed on the page? Has that sense of balance remained as her pictures develop?**

★ **Is he good with his hands? Was he quick to manage buttons or dress a teddy? The practical skills of drawing depend on practice, but they also need skilled hands.**

★ **Does the form and content of her pictures show unexpected maturity? For example, was she drawing faces before the age of three, while others of the same age were still scribbling? Do her pictures have more detail than those of her peers? By the age of five, do her pictures tell a story?**

★ **Has your child learned to draw to scale? Does she use perspective? Does she draw what she sees rather than what she knows?**

★ **Does she love drawing? Does she express her emotions in drawings? Are her drawings different when she is angry or sad? Does she turn to drawing to soothe or calm herself?**

★ **Does she experiment with colour and composition? Has she started to vary the orientation of her figures, so that people are not always staring directly out of the page? Does she draw happy and sad faces?**

# Getting ready to draw and paint

Drawing is wonderful practice for pen control, and for understanding how to translate an intention into a controlled action. It is also an enjoyable way to learn how to complete an activity, how to sit still and concentrate and how to create something others value.

## Before you start

**Children cannot enjoy painting and drawing if they are afraid to make a mess or of spilling things on their clothes. Your child needs an apron or painting smock and you need to set up a 'messy play' area.**

If you have a kitchen table this is ideal, otherwise cover a table and the adjoining surfaces with a wipe-clean table cover or sheets of newspaper. Alternatively, a small plastic table also provides a good surface. Paint needs to be thickened (see opposite) and put into a non-spill pot.

## What you can do

• To make a non-spill paint pot, cut out the middle section of a plastic bottle so that you are left with a beaker (the base) 10–12cm (4–5 inches) high and a neck section that is somewhat shorter. Put a few pebbles in the beaker for stability.

• Spread glue around the inside of the beaker rim and the outside base of the neck section. Invert the neck inside the beaker. Turn upside down and leave until the glue has dried. There should be a gap between the base and the bottom of the neck. Make up paint and fill. Use a cork to seal the pot between sessions.

• Set aside a time for messy play each day.

• Suggest that he uses soft crayons or coloured pencils for drawing instead, when there is not time to set up the messy corner.

• Encourage him to help to put things away.

## Brushes, pens and crayons

**If he wants to do something big and bold, he will need a big brush and a pot of paint, but when he wants to do something more detailed, crayons, pencils or felt-tip pens are more suitable. Chalks are good for using in the garden or for making temporary drawings on a slate.**

## What you can do

• Buy soft drawing pencils, stubby crayons, water-based felt-tips and short, fat brushes. Paste brushes are ideal.

• Provide a separate brush and pot for each colour. Do not bother with water (it increases the mess). Just clean brushes at the end of the session.

Your child can be imaginative with only a few colours.

## Paper and paint

Artshops have papers in a range of colours sold by the roll. For everyday drawings and paintings use old computer paper, the backs of circulars, or wallpaper. Check the absorbency. If it is too shiny the paint will not hold, if too absorbent the paper will rip. Buy powder paints, which are easier to use than blocks of colour. Your child will need only a few colours to create a wonderful variety of images.

## What you can do

• Thicken powder paint with soap flakes or cornflour.
• To make paint for a toddler, put a tablespoon of flour into a saucepan with a little water. Whisk and bring to the boil. Add food colouring.
• Old wallpaper works well for handprints – and footprints. Make up a bowl of powder paint, unroll the paper and let him step in the bowl and walk up and down on the paper. Definitely an outside game – have the hose ready to wash his feet before he comes inside.

# What the child learns

● Toddlers learn 'I did that – I made it happen'.

● If you put their paintings on the wall, they know you are pleased and their sense of achievement is boosted.

● Painting and drawing are excellent for developing hand–eye co-ordination.

● By the age of five or six, children learn to express emotions in their pictures.

● Drawing, in particular, is excellent practice in producing intended marks on the paper – something he will need to do when he starts to write.

● A child who has plenty of drawing practice is more likely to retain confidence in his artistic ability later on.

Abstract painting allows your child to be freely creative with colour.

• Give him a little bucket or an old paint tin and a decorator's paint brush. Let him 'paint' the garden fence or the outside of the wall with water.

• Fill an old washing-up liquid bottle with water and encourage him to 'draw' on the path or patio.

## Structured and free

**The most important lesson for toddlers and young children is that painting is fun. If they are to continue enjoying art through their school years and beyond, however, they must learn how to draw. When they are seven or eight years old, children start making representational drawings. They now know what they intend to draw or paint and if they feel they cannot achieve this they will give up, and sadly many do.**

## What you can do

• Provide colouring books and books of dot-to-dot drawings.

• Encourage your child to copy simple shapes by drawing around stencils, including tray puzzle pieces, plates, bricks or wooden shapes.

• Put a coin under a sheet of paper and make a coin rubbing with a soft pencil or a wax crayon. Try also rubbings of bark, embossed cards or wallpaper.

• Suggest that your older child copies simple drawings. Discuss what needs to be done to make the pictures more accurate.

• Introduce your child to mixed media. Your child can draw the easy shapes and stick cut-out photographs from magazines for other parts of the picture – for example, stick cut-out cars on roads, horses in fields, boats on the sea.

• Always encourage 'free drawing' alongside more structured lessons.

• Encourage older children to express how they feel by drawing or painting. For example, 'Make a picture of how angry/sad you are.'

# Drawing and painting activities

Drawing and painting offer some of the most important means of creative expression for young children. It is well worth offering your child the opportunity to experiment with a range of different materials and techniques.

## Making prints using potatoes, leaves and string

Even a two-year-old can make a potato print. Just dip a cut potato into a saucer of thickened paint (see page 37) and stamp it on to a piece of clean paper. Strings can be dipped into the paint and drawn across the paper to make squiggles. You can also make prints from leaves and cut fruit.

### What you can do
• Have a piece of newspaper handy to take the first print – it usually has too much paint on it.
• You can cut a pattern in a potato – or better still a turnip. Rotating the potato changes the pattern. Sponges can also be cut to shape.
• Dilute the paint or use paper of a different absorbency to alter the effect.
• Make handprints by putting hands on to a plate of paint and then on to a sheet of paper. Show her how to change the position of her fingers to make a different shape with them.

A two-year-old can make a potato print.

Even the youngest children will enjoy experimenting with colour and shape.

# What the child learns

● How to make wrapping paper or party invitations.

● An enhanced awareness of shape and spatial position.

● Good hand–eye co-ordination.

● To use nature and science as a source of inspiration.

● To ask questions and think of new solutions.

## Finger and sponge painting, splashing and blowing

These activities are suitable for very young children and provide messy fun for older ones. Children who have difficulty controlling their hands gain particular benefit. Pour paint directly on to a tray and swirl it on to a clean piece of paper.

### What you can do

• Finger painting. Put paints of different colours into little dishes. Show your child how to dip her finger in and then use her finger to paint with.

• Sponge or rag painting. Put paint on to a saucer. Give her a small piece of natural sponge or a piece of rag and show her how to dip it in and dab it on the paper.

• Blow painting. Show her how to blow through a straw. Make up some thin paint and drip it on to paper. Show her how to blow it into patterns using the straw.

• Making a print. Blow or spread paint on a table-top, tray or other hard, flat surface. Carefully lower absorbent paper on to the paint, remove and leave to dry.

• Make marbled paper by covering the base of a dish with a layer of home-made uncoloured flour paste. Drip a tablespoon of oil-based paint on to the surface. Swirl with a stick, place a piece of paper on top for 30 seconds and then remove.

• Dripping and flicking paint. The child dips the brush into the paint and lets it drip off on to the paper. Show her how to tap the brush. Make splatters by shaking or tapping the brush, or flicking the bristles with a finger.

## Folding paper and taking prints

Children over the age of three enjoy the element of surprise this activity offers. First fold a piece of paper down the middle, then open it out. Now put dabs of paint on to the paper. Refold the sheet and spread the paint by smoothing over the paper. Then open out the paper and see what design you have created.

### What you can do
• Use thickened paint in different colours for different effects.
• Let your child crease and smooth the paper herself.
• Experiment with glitter and home-made flour paste (see page 45).

## Using invisible ink

Older children enjoy sharing this activity with other children. Write a secret message or draw a picture by placing a sheet of paper rubbed with candle wax face down on another sheet of paper and write or draw firmly on the top sheet. Reveal the words or pictures by painting over the top of the message or picture.

Invisible ink or candle wax can be used in paintings as well as for writing secret messages.

### What you can do
• Try an alternative method of creating invisible writing. Let your child use potato or lemon juice to write the secret message. Warm it in a low oven to reveal the message 'as if by magic'.

## Templates and stencils

Bought stencils are easy to use and make attractive pictures. Your own templates are also simple to make. Show your child how to paint around the template and dab the spaces in the stencil.

### What you can do
• You can use real objects such as plates, a pair of scissors or leaves and templates. Or you could cut out pictures from magazines and use those instead.
• Alternatively, make your own from paper or card by cutting around objects and cutting out shapes.
• To make a simple stencil, fold a piece of paper into four and snip off the corners. Unfold to reveal the symmetrical pattern.

# Cutting and pasting

Cutting and pasting offer children a wide variety of creative opportunities – and plenty of practice in hand–eye co-ordination. Projects that involve cutting and pasting are among the best for helping a child learn to see an activity through from start to finish.

There are no limits to what your child can construct once she has learned to cut and paste.

## Breaking it down

Cutting out a paper shape and sticking it on another piece of paper is much too difficult for a three-year-old to manage without help. There are too many stages – selecting pictures, cutting them out, applying the glue and arranging the images on a sheet of paper. At this age he will enjoy each step for its own sake. As he develops he will continue to enjoy each stage and will gradually become more interested in the project as a whole. By the age of five or six, he may have a picture in mind before he starts, although he will sometimes change his plan later.

## Necessary skills

Cutting out a picture requires two skills: using scissors (which we can call learning to snip) and directing where those snips should be made (which we can call learning to cut – a far more sophisticated skill). Gluing is also more complex than it first seems. Glue has to be spread so it covers all areas that need sticking, while avoiding others. This can be difficult with a small cut-out. I find it easier to spread the glue on the paper and then to put on the cut-outs. Sprinkle the picture, for example with cocoa, flour or glitter, to cover any unsightly gluey areas and shake off the excess so that the picture re-emerges.

## What you can do

• Provide the right tools: small blunt-ended scissors, stubby paste brushes, glue with easy-to-use applicators such as roller balls, card or stiff paper that will not rip when it gets too wet.

• Provide the right structure. Let him snip first, then spread the glue. Do not necessarily get everything out at once. 'Tell me when you are ready for the glue' reminds him this is a staged activity.

• Make the task match his capabilities. If your three-year-old wants to stick people on his picture, cut them out for him.

• Be on hand to help if things go wrong.

• Display his creations on the wall or fix them on the refrigerator with a couple of strong magnets. It is the most effective praise you can give.

## Learning stage by stage

Introduce your child to cutting and pasting skills in graduated stages so that he is not put off by attempting a task that is too difficult for him.

**1** Ripping paper: start by teaching your child to rip narrow strips of paper. Then try ripping from a sheet in straight and curved lines. When he has gained confidence, help him to rip around shapes and then pictures.

**2** Snipping: start by helping your child to cut narrow strips of paper into short sections. Then progress to cutting along straight lines and then along curved lines. Then he will be ready to cut around easy shapes and later pictures.

**3** Gluing: start by teaching your child to apply glue to a sheet of paper so that he learns to cover the sheet. Then he can try putting glue on smaller pieces of paper. Once he can do this well, he is ready to put glue on the backs of pictures.

# Talent spotter

★ Good hand–eye co-ordination is essential for all craft skills. Does he build towers with his bricks that are taller than you would expect at his age? By the age of two was he able to place the last brick gently on top?

★ Was he able to use a crayon or pen before the age of two? Could he follow a line you had drawn by the time he was three? Does he enjoy joining up the dots and colouring in?

★ Does he choose activities that challenge his hand skills?

★ Did he cope with buttons and zippers at an early age (see Development Charts, pages 20–31)?

★ Is he able to twist his hand? Can he line up Lego pieces and undo screws?

★ Does he feed himself neatly for his age?

★ Is he good at recognizing and matching shapes? Does he enjoy jigsaw puzzles?

★ Is he unperturbed by drips of unwanted paste and misdirected snips?

★ Is he meticulous? Does he think before he acts?

# Snipping, ripping and dropping

Without practice, hands do not become skilled and children do not become organized. While we need to fit the materials to the child's current level of skill we also need to ensure she has some training for the next stage along the way.

## Learning to snip, rip and cut

Half the fun of using scissors is just to snip with them. Provided you supervise your child and have the right scissors – small and blunt-ended – even two-year-olds can try this. Make some long strips of paper about one 'snip' in width by cutting up glossy magazines. Show her how to snip across the strip.

## What the child learns

● **To control frustration when things go wrong.**

● **To become more organized and to start to plan.**

● **To work from start to finish.**

● **To sit still and concentrate.**

● **To feel good about her capabilities.**

## What you can do

• Once she has mastered snipping, she can start to cut thin card, newsprint, straws or even thin pasta and rice noodles.
• Increase the width of the strips to two snips and then three snips to cut across.
• Once she is confidently making successive snips, she is ready to learn how to cut but will need to build up other skills to cut accurately.
• Practise drawing around shapes, tracing and joining up dots.
• Show her how to rip newspaper. Draw a line and see if she can rip along it. Make it funny so mistakes do not matter. Gradually increase the difficulty so that she can rip around headlines, boxes and eventually photographs.
• Put the skills together. Show her how to cut along lines, around corners and eventually around shapes. Take it gradually and do not expect high levels of skill.

Pasting and dropping can be used to make attractive gifts.

Once your child has mastered snipping, she can progress to more complex shapes.

## Making and spreading paste

Flour paste is simple to make. Take a handful of plain flour, a pinch of salt and add water slowly, stirring all the time. When it is gooey it is ready. A slightly stronger version can be made by adding enough water to half a cup of flour to make a mixture as thick as single cream. Simmer for five minutes, stirring constantly. You can add a few drops of food colouring to either type of paste. Store in a jar in the fridge.

Paste is good for sticking paper and other lightweight materials, but if you need it to hold something heavier you should use glue. PVA (polyvinyl acetate) is the best commercial glue for children to use. It is non-toxic, can be wiped off most surfaces when wet and peeled off many when dry. (If it gets on to clothes and you cannot pick it off, put the clothes in the freezer and try again while they are frozen). The hand-washing gel that garage mechanics use to remove grease also works well.

### What you can do

• At first let her apply the paste however she likes. Later teach her to spread the glue evenly.

• Spread the glue and then cover part of the area before sprinkling on your first 'drop'. Then choose another material to drop on to the area you had previously covered up.

• Mask part of the surface by placing a cup or plate on the paper and then spread glue around. This means that the dropped items will stick only to the glued area.

**Your child will enjoy dropping objects on to glue to see the effect.**

## What you can do
• Keep a store of materials for dropping. Useful items include: used ground coffee and dried coffee powder or granules, tea leaves, egg shells, seeds, rice, dried beans and lentils, pasta shapes, snipped paper and fabric, cotton wool, sand, sequins, glitter.
• On outings look for some special 'drops': leaves, petals, bark, sheep's wool, feathers, bus tickets and seed heads.

## Dropping rice
Children of all ages will enjoy this activity. Younger ones will need supervision but older children can be left to get on with the various projects by themselves.

### What you can do
• Cover the paper or card with glue and then drop rice on to the card. Let it dry flat, then shake off any excess rice and display on the wall.
• Alternatively, draw a daisy with a ring of petals. Carefully paste each petal and drop the rice. Shake off any excess, then cut out a circle from yellow paper and stick it in the middle.
• Take a piece of coloured paper. Write the child's name on the paper with glue. Let her sprinkle the rice and reveal her name.
• Place a saucer or a cup as a template on a piece of paper. Carefully spread glue around it, covering all the paper that is showing. Remove the template and drop the rice. When this is dry, put glue in the area left by the template and drop something else – cocoa powder, instant coffee or split peas, for example.

## Dropping
All sorts of things can be dropped or placed on a ready-glued surface, either randomly or in patterns. For a simple drop all you need to do is cover the page with glue and drop whatever you have in mind. Then shake off the excess (if she is using a heavy 'drop' such as noodles and split peas let the glue dry first) before putting it on the wall. Light materials such as paper, glitter, cocoa, grass cuttings and flower petals will stick to flour paste. Heavier drops such as lentils need PVA glue.

# Making collages, cards and masks

These are activities that need planning and supervision. The first step is to decide what you will make, then you can gather the materials.

## Making cards and invitations

Home-made Christmas or birthday cards from a child are always charming. The easiest Christmas cards to make use cut-outs from last year's cards or a seasonal but simple design such as that made by sticking gold stars on a dark blue background. A collage of strips of marbled paper (see page 40) can also be highly decorative.

Use similar techniques to produce cards and invitations for a variety of occasions, including birthdays and get-well cards. Your child will learn that people value his home-made efforts more than they would a shop-bought item. He will also learn that he can contribute to festivities and special occasions like anyone else.

Home-made cards are quick and easy to make.

### What you can do

• If you have a computer, help your child to compose a message or greeting, print it out and stick it inside your cards.
• Make place-setting cards and dinner menus. For example, involve him in the preparation for special family events. This can be a help to you if you are busy with other tasks.

## Mixed media

Collage – the deliberate placing of items in a specific place in the picture – can be used in conjunction with more random dropping techniques (see page 46). Collage can also be combined with drawing, painting and many other techniques.

**Supervision may limit the mess that can result from collage-making!**

**The bigger the features, the more impressive the mask will be.**

## What you can do

• Start by drawing a picture, then add cut-outs from comics and magazines.
• Make greetings cards using string painting. Dip a piece of string into paint and pull it over the paper.
• Combine leaf prints with leaves and flowers; a background of potato prints and a foreground of felt shapes.
• Add cotton wool and glitter to a paint-splattered background.

## Making masks

Mask-making is a good project for Halloween or for a 'monster play'. You can hang them outside your child's door to frighten the scary things that come in the night. Masks help to conquer fears by encouraging your child to laugh and play with things that frighten him. A simple mask can be made using a paper bag. Just put it over his head and mark the position of the eyes and, after taking it off, cut out the eyeholes. You can also make masks from card or paper plates.

## What you can do

• Decorate a paper bag (never plastic) with a face. Add strands of wool for hair, eyelashes and eyebrows. You can cut out a big mouth from sticky-backed paper.
• Make a big head from card. First roll it into a cylinder so that it goes over the face and around the side of the head. Secure with tape or elastic. Make the eyeholes in the mask's mouth so the face is very big and impressive and stands up above the child's head. Make a nose and eyes from strips of newspaper, wool or cotton wool. Use a crayon to draw in eyelashes and the mouth.
• Use paper plates to make simple faces. Use crayons, collage or a combination of the two to create the features on the face.

# What the child learns

- The child learns to work towards a specific goal.

- Boosts confidence and a sense of achievement.

- That he can sit and concentrate while still having fun.

- Provides a sustained activity that he can break from and return to.

- Practice in working alone sometimes, but also in asking for help when he needs it.

- Good for hand–eye co-ordination.

## A simple collage

First decide what you are going to make. Outdoor scenes are often a good choice because you can use materials that are easily available. A snow scene, for example, could be created with cotton wool, pictures of skiers and mountains cut from travel magazines. You could make a house from off-cuts of cloth, a roof from straw and a sandpaper garden path. You will need to draw an outline of the scene on some paper or card. Gather together everything you need, including paste or glue, but do not give him all the materials at once. He may just want to stick things where he wants and admire the result.

### What you can do

• Use papers of different colours. Choose a dark colour for a night scene, yellow or blue for a beach scene, green if there is to be a lot of grass.
• Make sure that the glue you are using is strong enough to stick all the materials you have chosen. If there are any items that may be problematic, offer your child some help, for example, by providing some stronger glue.
• If he is happily working on his own, give him advice only when asked. Praise what he has done when he starts to look like he is being distracted.
• If he is working to a plan, discuss this at the start and remind him of his original intention as he goes along.
• Filling in a picture can be time-consuming, so be prepared to spread the task over a few days.

# Modelling clay and dough

Children love the feel of modelling materials. If you give your child a ball of clay and a blunt knife, she will cut, roll and poke the surface. But small children spend as much time simply handling the material as shaping it.

## Handling materials

Once a child is able to use her fingers and thumbs in opposition (by the end of the first year), she starts to interact with objects in a variety of ways. Once she swiped, grabbed and banged toys; now she picks things up between finger and thumb, and pushes, pulls, drops, turns over and later places toys where she wants them to be. Alongside this increased skill in manipulating objects, there is a change in the way she first explores them. Whereas once everything went first to the child's mouth, objects are now patted, poked, stroked or squeezed. When children first encounter modelling materials, it is this sort of exploration that predominates. The activity is as much (or more) about how things feel than what can be made.

Children love modelling clay from a very early age, and by five, most can construct satisfying objects.

## Simply explore

Because they are just starting to feel, two-year-olds adore the slippery feel of damp clay (but beware, it is messy) or newspaper that has been shredded, soaked in water and the excess water squeezed out. Less messy materials include a bowl of rice or sugar that she can run through her fingers, or a paste of cornflour and water she can stir (put it in a baking tray and add a drop of food colouring or blackcurrant juice).

For this age group, make flour dough with a little extra oil. Mix it in a saucepan and heat it gently so that it is warm and slightly gooey. Dry sand flows pleasingly, wet sand can be squeezed and moulded. Both can be used indoors if you have a large groundsheet or a suitable area with a washable floor. A mixing bowl half-filled with sand is enough.

## Materials for temporary models

Clay is wonderful to handle but can make a lot of mess. Unless you have a dedicated play space, it is definitely a special treat material. It is wonderful to play with it on the terrace or garden path in warm weather. Play dough is probably the best everyday modelling material for a small child. Plasticine is harder to get out of the carpet, but small pieces keep their shape, allowing your child to make more detailed models.

## Making lasting models

Unless you can fire them in a kiln, clay models become fragile when dry. It may be more practical to break them down and roll the clay back into the ball at the end of the session. If your child wants to make a model she can keep, try papier-mâché or salt dough – or obtain a supply of one of the proprietary modelling materials designed to be baked in a domestic oven.

# Talent spotter

★ Does she seem to enjoy the feel of different materials?

★ Does she place her drawings or scribbles well on the page and so that there is as much on one side of the page as the other? Has that sense of balance remained as her pictures have developed?

★ Does she have good spatial skills? For example, does she build towers with bricks that are taller than you would expect for her age?

★ Does she choose activities that challenge her hand skills?

★ Is she good at recognizing and matching shapes? Does she enjoy jigsaw puzzles? Did she start playing with them before the age of three?

★ Are construction kits among her favourite toys? Children who 'see' how things fit together find it easier to work with 3D models.

★ Does she make things without being asked? Does she choose to model rather than paint?

★ Does she include detail in her models – for example, putting eyes on snakes?

★ Is her modelling mature for her age? Most children under four just feel the clay rather than making anything from it.

# Play dough, salt dough, papier mâché

It is always good to have some ideas for special activities on a rainy day. The great thing about making play dough, salt dough or papier mâché is that we usually have all the ingredients at hand.

## Play dough

You can buy play dough, but it is very easy – and much cheaper – to make. The basic recipe is two cups of flour, one cup of salt, two tablespoons of oil, one cup of water and a little food colouring. You can make it in a bread-maker or food processor, or simply mix by hand and then knead. Finally warm the dough in a large saucepan (or a low oven) until you have a soft lump. You can make dough without oil or heating it, but the dough is less silky. If you add a little more oil it feels even softer.

Add the food colouring to the mixing water for a uniform colour, or add at the final kneading stage for a marbled effect. Or you could do both – for example, mix yellow colouring into the water and add red to the mix for yellow dough marbled in red and orange. Adding two teaspoons of cream of tartar helps keep the dough in good condition between sessions. Store in an airtight bag or plastic box. If it seems dry when you get it out, dip it in oily water, knead and then warm.

## What you can do

• Use different textures of dough and let your young child squeeze, cut and roll.
• Show your child how to make impressions in the dough with coins, toys, leaves or pebbles.
• Use pastry or cookie cutters to make shapes or cut around shapes with a plastic knife.
• Roll two colours together to make a striped snake.
• Play dough is good for making casts – for example, of hands and feet. Just roll out a thick piece of dough and help him to press his hand or foot into it. Leave to dry and harden over a few days.

## Salt dough

Salt dough dries to a harder finish than play dough and can be used to make models that will last. To make the dough, mix three cups of plain flour, one cup of salt, a little over one cup of water and a tablespoon of glycerin (available from pharmacies or drug stores). Knead until the dough is elastic in texture. Once formed into shapes you

Once they are baked, dough models will last for a long time.

can bake it hard. Place the item on a tray lined with baking parchment or foil. Put in an oven preheated to 150°C (300°F). Thin items take about an hour and a half to bake, thicker models take longer. If the item starts to brown, turn down the heat of the oven. Once cool, a hardened salt dough model can be simply varnished, or painted using poster paints prior to varnishing.

**What you can do**
• Make brightly coloured or fun-shaped buttons for his coat.
• Make a name plate for his door.
• Make plates and pretend food for the doll's house.
• Make brooches and badges (stick a safety pin in the back before cooking).
• Make beads by rolling the dough around thick, metal knitting needles that you have oiled. Stick the needles into a large potato to dry upright in the oven.
• Make monsters, Christmas decorations (do not forget a hole for the string) or

# What the child learns

● He can easily produce satisfactory results alone and this builds confidence.

● To do things with you and create things that will last.

● Dough provides lots of creative scope for 'What happens if …?' and 'I did that' activities.

● Sitting still and focusing on manipulating the dough is great practice for the concentration needed for more challenging activities when he is older.

**Play dough is a good substitute for clay.**

half and sew up the seam. Cut off the top corner so that it fits the neck and glue in place. wrap wool around the fabric to secure the neck and hide the join.

## Papier mâché

Tear half a dozen newspapers into thin strips. Put them into a plastic bowl and pour on hot water. Make sure all the paper is wet. Leave for several hours. Knead into a mushy texture, then squeeze out the excess water. Dilute PVA glue (three parts water to one part glue) or make flour paste (see page 45) and mix into the paper mush. The mixture should be as stiff as clay or plasticine. If it is too sloppy, squeeze out the moisture again.

### What you can do
• Papier mâché can be used like clay to make pots, people, animals and doll's furniture. Because it is cheap, it is ideal for big models.
• It can also be moulded. Invert a bowl and cover it with a layer of plastic wrap or petroleum jelly. Now spread a layer of papier mâché over the bowl and leave for 24 hours to dry. Repeat with more layers for a sturdier bowl. Remove from the mould when the final layer is dry.
• Balloons can be used as moulds to make papier mâché heads. Pop the balloon when the papier mâché is dry. Use wire frames to make more complex creatures.

chopstick rests. These can be painted with powder paint and varnished when dry, or you could even use some clear nail polish.
• Make a cast of his hand or foot. Line the base of a loose-bottomed cake tin, put in the dough, pat smooth, then press his hands or feet into the dough. Bake them in the oven and then varnish.
• Make a small doll by rolling a ball of salt dough and forming it into a head. Take a second smaller ball and roll this to form the neck. Attach to the head by dampening the surfaces. Bake. To make the body, cut a semi-circle of fabric, fold in

# Using bought materials

From sand to ready-to-roll pastry, there are lots of materials you can buy that your child can use for modelling. Some of the results can be eaten, some make permanent decorations and some are just fun to make.

## Food

Cooking often involves mixing, cutting and moulding, and children are usually more than willing to help. Preparing the bread for a traditional bread pudding is rather like making papier mâché. Just soak slices of bread in a mixture of milk, eggs and spice. Squeeze out the excess mixture and place the bread in a buttered dish in layers sprinkled with currants. Bake in a moderate oven. You could also introduce your child to that favourite cooking activity of mixing cake batter. With cooking activities there is always the added treat of eating what you have made.

Playing with edible materials provides an introduction to cooking and food preparation.

## What you can do

• Use marzipan to make animals (paint them with food colouring).
• Cut out gingerbread men and give them currant eyes.
• Cut stars from ready-to-roll icing to decorate a cake (white stars look great on dark blue icing) or make pastry shapes to decorate a pie.
• Mix a can of tuna into cooled mashed potatoes. Add salt, pepper, and an egg. Form into patties, coat in breadcrumbs and fry.

• Let your child mix a rice or couscous salad with clean hands.
• Roll out puff pastry, cut out shapes and bake in a hot oven. Pile up the cooked shapes with jam.

# What the child learns

● To enjoy working with others, to be helpful, to believe everyone should do some of the chores.

● To mix and mould carefully and work towards an end.

● To use her imagination to make her own world.

● To do things with you and create things that will last or give pleasure to others.

## Fimo

This is pliable material that can be baked in an oven to make durable ornaments and jewellery. It comes in a wide variety of colours, which can be mixed to give marbled finishes.

### What you can do
• Older children can follow the instructions to make quite elaborate models, but most younger children are content to make simple shapes, buttons, brooches and earrings. Varnish the items after baking.
• Look out for kits that contain fixings and fastenings. The professional finish is particularly pleasing for your child. Mix and marble colours together.

## Bird cake

Making a feed block for garden birds is one of the easiest kitchen games, involving moulding soft materials. It also encourages your child to watch wildlife and to develop her powers of observation while identifying birds that come to feed. An older child might like to keep a diary of these visitors.

To make the cake, help your child to mix a variety of seeds, dried fruit, breadcrumbs and suet in a bowl. Melt some lard in a pan and pour it over the mixture, but do this yourself – do not allow a young child to handle hot fat. Your child can mix with a spoon. If it is all absorbed and the mixture seems dry, add a little more melted fat. Again, do this yourself.

Once the mixture is cool enough to handle, show her how to knead it. Let her enjoy the process. Press the mixture into old yogurt pots or similar containers. Use a stick or skewer to push a string into the middle of the mixture and press the pudding down firmly. Melt a little more fat, and pour it over the top so the string will be held firmly. Put the cake in the fridge to set. Carefully remove from the pot and hang where it can be seen from the window. Wait for birds to feed.

## What you can do

• Add chopped bacon to the mix.
• Look up the different birds you see in a reference book and teach your child their names.
• Keep a record in a special book or diary of the birds that visit.

## The sandpit

Sand is a wonderful substance. It flows like water when it is dry. When it is wet, you can mould it into puddings and pies, build roads for toy cars or construct castles. Sand is the perfect 'I made it happen' toy. Anyone can play and anyone can decide what to play. It does not confine. You can make a simple sandpit from a large plastic bowl, or contain the sand in a wooden or brick-built frame outside. Buy soft, pre-washed sand. Protect your sandpit from cats: they will use it as a dirt tray unless you cover it.

## What you can do

• Provide a bucket and spade, some moulds, a rake, and perhaps a colander for your child to use in the sandpit. Plastic mugs and bowls are also useful.
• Give your child a bowl of dry sand, a funnel, a cup, a colander, and fine and coarse sieves and let them explore.
• Give your child an assortment of jugs, bowls and cups and ask her to find out which holds the most sand.
• Flags, lollipop sticks and shells are good for decorating castles.
• Few people have the sort of home that easily accommodates an indoor sand pit, but a bowl of soft sand can be enjoyed by a young child in an easily cleaned 'messy' corner of the house.
• Fill a bag with dry sand, cut the corner off the bag, and let the child 'draw' with the stream of sand.
• Buy a water wheel and pour the sand through it.

Provide children with a range of 'tools' to use with sand or other bought materials.

# Craft activities

Young children love making things. The things they make do not need to be useful or decorative – the pleasure is mostly in the making. Whether a product of his imagination or the result of following instructions, making things is wonderful practice for sitting still, concentrating and working towards a goal.

## Learning by example

Children have always learned basic craft skills by watching and joining in – so do not be afraid to do rather more than help in the beginning. The progression for a simple craft activity, such as making pasta jewellery, should be that when the child is two, you make things with his help, at three you make them together, from four to five he makes things with your help and by six he works alone with occasional assistance. For something more complex like sewing, knitting or carpentry, the starting age is later but the basic pattern remains the same: he helps, you share, you help, you then remain in the background to advise when necessary.

All children will be proud of something they have made themselves.

## Selecting a craft

Because children imitate their parents, the first choice of craft for them is the one that you enjoy. They will learn to sew if you teach them, but they are more likely to love sewing if you clearly enjoy it too. If you cannot set a good example (and these days most of us cannot) select something that interests him – like making toys, or sewing a new costume for the dressing-up box. At Christmas and around birthdays, making presents is always a good starting point for craft activities.

## Gifts from the heart

When he presents you with a pair of earrings he has made, he does so with pride. When you receive them lovingly and wear them, you reinforce that pride. Making something for someone has always had a particular value in Western culture. It is easy to forget that children also express their creativity within loving social relationships.

## Preparation

Even if he is only making a snake from sections of cardboard tubes or some jewellery from pasta, craft activities need organization. Crafts usually have more than one stage – making and decorating or cutting out and sewing – which demands orderly planning and organization. Young children find it hard to plan, so you will need to do most of it for him. However, you can involve him in your plans, for example by asking if there is anything else you need and ticking off lists. Put everything he needs on a table to prevent him knocking things over or stepping on them. A large kitchen table is ideal for crafts, but if this is not possible, set up a messy corner with a plastic sheet and a table and chair that can be easily wiped clean. Plastic garden furniture is a practical option.

## What you can do

• Show by example when you can.
• Create a special space for craft activities. If you do not have a suitable kitchen table, consider getting a small plastic garden table for him to use.
• Prepare for mess. If necessary, protect furniture and clothing.
• Find time. Craft activities are not something to amuse your child while you get on with your own things.
• Know when to let go. You may be in charge in the first months but gradually you have to pass the control to him.
• Use your imagination; adapt and build on activities you have done before.
• Receive gifts with gratitude and display them with pride. If you take off the earrings he made when you leave the house, put them on again before you meet up again at the end of the day – he will notice.

# Talent spotter

★ Does he build towers with his bricks that are taller than you would expect for his age?

★ Are his eating and dressing skills advanced for his age (see the Development Charts, pages 20–31)?

★ Are his drawing skills advanced? For example, was he able to use a crayon or pen before he was two? Could he follow a line you had drawn by the time he was three? By the age of four, did he enjoy dot-to-dot and colouring-in?

★ Is his drawing neater than that of other children his age?

★ Does he choose activities that challenge his hand skills?

★ Is he meticulous? Does he think before he acts?

★ Does he have well-developed fine motor skills? For example, did he cope with buttons and zippers before the age of four?

★ Is he good at recognizing and matching shapes? For example, does he enjoy jigsaw puzzles?

★ Is he well organized?

★ Does he enjoy making things?

# Making dolls and animals

There is always room for a few extra play people in her games. Once you have taught her how to make dolls, she may do it for the simple pleasure of creating them.

## Cloth dolls

These little dolls were always a favourite with my children. To make them you need a piece of cloth about 12 x 15cm (4 x 6 inches). A scrap from an old sheet is ideal. You will also need a cotton wool ball and some wool or string. Put the cloth on the table and roll both of the long edges in towards the centre – leaving a section in the middle that is big enough to hold the cotton wool ball. You should now have two tubes of cloth with a flat section between them.

Put the cotton wool ball about two thirds of the way up this flat section and fold the top down over the ball. Use the string to fix the cotton wool in place by tying under the ball to make a head and neck and turn the doll over. Do not cut the ends off the string.

Pull out the arms (the shorter rolled sections) and cross the string across the doll's back and tie around the waist. If she is a girl doll just roll up her skirt a little and use two more bits of string to tie off her feet. Later you can make her a

## What the child learns

● To pay attention, sit still, concentrate and persist with an activity from start to finish.

● To listen, follow instructions and work with others.

● To take pride in what she makes and gain confidence.

● To perfect her skills gradually so that she can do more of the activity without help.

● Playing with play people encourages her to talk for them and helps her to think through social situations.

simple dress or a headscarf if you want to. If it is a boy doll, cut the material between the legs and tie off. Draw in the face. You can also make larger dolls from tea towels in the same way.

## What you can do
• Make dolls for your Christmas tree with red, green or gold cloth. For a festive look, try putting PVA on the dress and shaking glitter over it.
• Make simple aprons for dolls. Stick on woollen hair with PVA glue.
• Buy some furry cloth to make animals.
• People can also be made from coloured pipe cleaners. You can use one pipe cleaner to make the head, body and legs and a shorter section to make the arms.
• Draw a face on a 'dolly' clothes peg. Glue hair in place (or ears or a hat) and dress with scraps of cloth.

## Snakes

A basic snake is easy to make. You just need a length of string, six toilet-roll tubes (or for a larger version paper-towel tubes) and some tape. He will probably want to decorate the tubes first. He can paint or draw scales on to the tubes.

Alternatively, you can help him to roll each tube in paper or pretty cloth, which you can secure with PVA or tape. Do not forget to put some eyes on the last tube. Making up the snake is simple. Pass the string through the first tube and then double back around the tube and tie to the other end of the string. Secure the remaining tubes in the same way, making sure there is enough string left to pull the snake along. Make a loop in the end of the string to form the pulling handle.

Cloth and clothes peg dolls are easy and fun to make.

A carer's time and patience in helping a child with a project such as this is well rewarded by the pleasure and stimulus that the finished object provides.

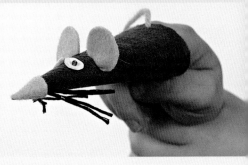

Once your child has made his puppet he can use it for creative play.

## What you can do

• Work with your child. He can decorate and thread the tubes on to the string, but you will need to tie the knots for him.

• Help him make some cardboard fangs for the head. Just glue them in place with PVA.

• You can make tiny snakes with pasta tubes or cotton spools. Make enormous ones from cylindrical biscuit packages.

• You can make a friendly monster using a small box for the head and a larger one for the body. Stick four matchboxes on to the bigger box to make the legs and a toilet roll tube to make a tail.

## Making puppets

Making puppets can be as easy or as complex as you like. For example, a sock simply needs a face, and the sleeve of an old jumper needs a knot in the end and a face. If your child places his thumb opposite his fingers he can use its big mouth to 'speak'.

## What you can do

• Draw a body without any legs on some stiff card. Mark two holes near the base of the body so that your child can poke her fingers through to make the legs. You could make an elephant with one hole and poke a finger through for the trunk.

• Cut the top off a bottle so that you are left with a tube that can be decorated. Add a face and some hair or a hat and ears. The puppet sits on your child's hand and wrist and he can bob it up and down as the puppet speaks.

• Twist the corners of a paper bag to make ears and draw on a face.

• Stick two paper plates together (eating surfaces facing each other) leaving a gap on one side big enough for the child's hand. Paint a face, stick or staple on wool for hair, add a hat or a cork nose. The child can just slip their hand between the plates and is ready to play.

# Decorating clothes and jewellery

Whether it is party time or just a wet afternoon, all children enjoy having a new outfit. Next time the rain keeps you in the house, why not make one together?

## Pasta jewellery

Pasta comes in a wide variety of shapes – bows, shells and tubes – and in a range of sizes. Pasta tubes are most suitable for necklaces, but almost any shape can be used for brooches and earrings. You can paint the shapes (let one side dry before turning over to paint the other) using poster paints. Once the paint is dry, varnish the jewellery with clear nail polish. Use a bodkin to thread pasta tubes on strings or elastic thread to make bracelets and necklaces.

## What you can do

• Use painted pasta shapes to decorate boxes or picture frames.
• If you want to thread pasta shapes other than tubes, cook them until they are almost soft and then thread them on a piece of string. Put the pasta on a baking tray lined with baking parchment into a low oven (150°C/300°F) for an hour. If it starts to brown, turn the heat down. When the pasta is dry and hard, paint and varnish as usual. You can also put earring clips or hooks into part-cooked pasta.

Pasta is not just for cooking; coloured and strung together it can also make a fun necklace.

layers into the shape of brooch you require. Turn over and attach the safety pin to the back. Arrange the pressed flowers on the brooch. Put a small dab of PVA underneath each flower. Spray with hair spray (for safety, you should do this yourself). If you want to wear it more than once or twice, you will need to cover the flower with sellotape or plastic.

## What you can do

• Use small shells or sequins to decorate a brooch. They will last longer than flowers. Painted pasta shapes work well too.

• Use pressed flowers to make birthday cards and to decorate place-setting cards for a special party.

• Help your child to stick pressed flowers into a scrapbook. Record the flower's name, the date it was collected and where it was found.

• Decorate a plastic belt by sticking on pressed flowers, sequins or shells.

## New clothes for old

An easy way to remodel a pair of jeans is with paint. Buy trial pots of emulsion paint and a small roller. Cover the floor and table with newspaper. Lay out the jeans and pour a little emulsion on to a plate. Show your child how to roll the roller in the paint, make a first roll on to paper to get rid of the excess paint. Then roll on to the leg of the jeans. Two or three thick lines down the thigh area of each leg looks good. You could use contrasting colours and scatter a little glitter over the paint while it is still wet. Leave it to dry.

To tie-dye a shirt you will need fabric dye and rubber bands or string. Wrap sections of material with bands or string

Leaves also make attractive brooches.

## Making a pressed flower brooch

Flowers can be pressed in a special press or in a heavy book between two sheets of blotting paper. Put the blotting paper in the book and lay out the flower in an attractive way, cover with a second piece of paper and close the book. Leave for a few weeks.

To make the brooch, you will need a piece of card, a small piece of velvet, a safety pin and some PVA glue. Help your child spread PVA over the card and stick the card and velvet together. Cut both so areas of the material are completely covered. Dye the garment using cold- or warm-water dyes according to the manufacturer's instructions. Remove the bands and strings after rinsing the clothes through thoroughly.

**What you can do**
• An alternative way to decorate jeans is to apply emulsion paint using the dripping technique (see page 40). Be careful to protect your surfaces and be sure to wipe away all the stray splatters before they dry.
• You can buy special fabric paints to draw on old T-shirts. You could also sponge, flick or drip paint onto the cloth.
• Stick glitter or sequins to a T-shirt or jeans using PVA. Just apply the glue and drop the glitter into place. Hand-wash carefully.
• Make a very thick paste of flour and water (see page 45) and let your child use this to paint on an old white T-shirt. Let it dry completely. Put cold-water dye in the soap tray of your washing machine and wash on a cold wash cycle, then wash with detergent on a warm cycle to remove the paste and reveal your design.
• If you dye material with a light colour, the whole process can then be repeated with second colour over the top.

Older children will love to give their worn clothes a makeover.

# What the child learns

● **Excellent for improving fine-finger skills and developing hand–eye co-ordination.**

● **Encourages your child to sit and concentrate – an essential skill for school.**

● **Gives your child pride in what they do.**

# Cardboard constructions

Cardboard boxes of every size hold a fascination for young children. They sit in them, pull them along, hide things in them, but most of all they enjoy building them into fabulous constructions.

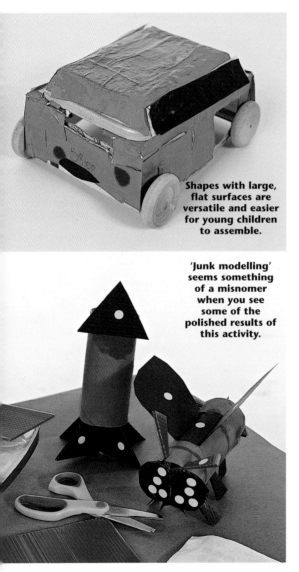

**Shapes with large, flat surfaces are versatile and easier for young children to assemble.**

**'Junk modelling' seems something of a misnomer when you see some of the polished results of this activity.**

## Art and craft

Construction can be free – dictated only by the materials and the builder's imagination – or it can be structured – directed by a plan. Children should be encouraged to build in both ways, because each teaches very different skills. Free construction, like free painting, is about seeing what she can do, about playing with the materials and, later, about expressing herself in funny and clever ways.

Building specific objects is more of a craft. Even before she picks up her glue brush, she knows where she is heading and what she needs to include. When she sets out to make a car from a big box and some paper plates, she knows certain things about cars – that they have wheels, for example – and she looks at the available materials with this in mind. Referring to the activity as 'making a car' helps her keep the picture of the finished product in mind. Calling the plates 'wheels' leaves no doubt about where they should go.

## Just building

A young child does not need to work out why two things can be stuck together. The answer is obvious to her – it is because she has put glue on them. She does not take into account, for example, how much of the glued surface is in contact – as older children and adults do. She cannot think in a logical way or consider that there might be more than one reason why something happens.

She will be less frustrated if you stick with simple shapes for her first constructions. Tubes can be difficult to stick at first – however you place a tube, there is never much of it in contact with a box or a second tube. The best way to stick a tube vertically to a surface is to make five or six small cuts in the base of the tube and bend back the card between cuts to make flaps. She now has a surface on which to put the glue. For even greater stability, glue – or better still – staple the flaps to a flat piece of card. You will need to prepare both ends of some tubes so she can use them as pillars. If you call the 'one-ended' tubes chimneys and the 'two-ended' tubes pillars it will help her remember which she should use for which purpose.

## What you can do

• Collect cardboard boxes and tubes in a range of sizes.
• Prepare a suitable space that is large enough for the activity.
• Make time to help your child. A young child needs you to work with her, an older child needs you to be available for support and advice.
• Let her decide on the project. Sometimes you can make a suggestion for something special, at other times let her make what she wants to make. If she needs help, give it, but as she grows up you should pass control over to her.
• Show your pride in her achievements. Display her creations for all to admire.

# Talent spotter

★ Does she enjoy making things?

★ Are her eating and dressing skills advanced for her age (see the Development Charts, pages 20–31)?

★ Does she enjoy construction kits?

★ Can she sit still and concentrate? If distracted does she go back to what she was doing?

★ Can she follow instructions well for her age? Children under seven cannot follow a string of instructions, but a two- to three-year-old may be able to follow them one at a time.

★ Is she happy to get messy?

★ Is she meticulous? Does she think before she acts? By the age of four can she plan one step ahead?

★ Is she good at recognizing and matching shapes? Does she prefer construction kits (where she can decide where to place pieces) to jigsaw puzzles where there is only one correct place?

★ Is she patient? Can she cope if things do not immediately fit where she wants them to go? Does she ask for advice when she is uncertain?

★ Is she able to twist her hand? Can she line up Lego pieces and undo screws?

# Just constructing

Little boxes can be turned into houses or a station for a railway, medium boxes into a doll's house, a café or a fire station. Boxes big enough to climb into become cars, trains or planes. It is just a matter of getting the right props and adding the finishing touches.

Brick-based kits are good for building realistic constructions.

## Over-the-counter construction kits

If your child loves constructing, he may benefit from a shop-bought kit. There is an ever-expanding range, including kits based on bricks where the pieces are lined up and pushed together. These come with pieces of various sizes. Small hands need big pieces. Other kits have pieces that join at various points and do not need to be lined up accurately – these are best for very young children. There are also kits based on the principle of popping beads, and those that have rods and separate fixtures, and make more 'engineering' constructions. If a child really enjoys constructing he will want one of each sort.

### What you can do
• Construction kits do not suit all children, so try him with a starter kit first.
• Provide a quiet room.
• If he likes to build realistically, he may prefer the bricks. If he likes to make large constructions, he may prefer the rods and fixtures or some of the kits that use a popping bead system.
• If he doesn't play with the kit, put it away and bring it out later. We sometimes

# What the child learns

● Develops the ability to concentrate on a single activity.

● Encourages spatial skills and fine finger skills.

● Offers opportunities to use his imagination and engage in make-believe.

● Helps your child learn when to ask for help.

● Communication, social skills and cooperation.

● Promotes practical skills of balancing, sticking and fixing.

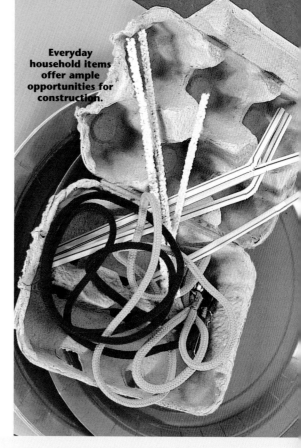

Everyday household items offer ample opportunities for construction.

introduce complicated kits too soon. Be guided by the age on the box.
• If your child likes constructing, give him a range of kits.

## Collection box

Most households throw away a huge amount of packaging that can be used for creative constructions. Look for a wide range of sizes and shapes from matchboxes to cereal packages. Avoid anything that is flimsy or that will be difficult to stick to another surface. Check that margarine tubs and yogurt pots do not have a lipped base – they need to sit flush with the adjoining surface. Paper plates and plastic pot lids make excellent wheels.

## What you can do
• Use PVA glue to fasten flat surfaces together.
• Fix wheels with split pins, which leave them free to turn.
• When necessary, use staples or rubber bands to hold sections in place until the glue dries.
• Sticky-backed plastic can be difficult for a child to handle but sometimes nothing else will do.
• Double-sided foam sticking pads can often work when glue is not suitable.
• If an item is impossible to cut with blunt-ended scissors, do the cutting for him with a sharp pair of scissors.
• Use only short lengths of string to avoid any risk of strangulation.

A road layout can combine a range of bought materials and home-made props.

## Making a pull-along toy

It is difficult for a child without young brothers and sisters to cope with a visiting toddler. Get him in the mood by helping him make a present for a younger visitor. Part-fill a large plastic bottle with painted pasta. Make a hole in the lid, put a string through and knot to make a handle.

### What you can do

• Making presents is always a good idea for a child who prefers making things to playing with them.
• Use the toyshop for inspiration. Look at the toys on offer and consider how you might make your own versions of them.

## A road layout for a rainy day

There are certain store-cupboard constructions that become permanent toys which can be put away between games and added to from time to time. A road layout is one of them. Roads are easily made from postcards, index cards or the edges of cereal boxes. Let your child help you paint them black and,

when dry, add road markings with white nail polish or gloss paint. You can make traffic circles and squares, and even cobbled streets. Make houses and shops from boxes, pavement cafés from matchboxes and cocktail umbrellas. He just has to add toy cars and some pipe-cleaner people (see page 61).

### What you can do

• Make trees from toilet-roll tubes. Tape two or three together, make long cuts in the top one and fold down the flaps to make branches. Stick on paper leaves or dye some cotton wool green and stick it on.
• Paint large sheets of cardboard green to make lawns and parks.
• Make or buy road signs and cars.
• Use the houses and roads for a variety of different layouts – for example, arrange them to make a village, a farm or a railway.

# Creating a world of their own

When children play, they either act out a game, or they make their toys act out the game, rather like telling a story. Whether you make life-size props for these games or make characters for the story may depend on what you have to hand.

## Making a doll's house

Wine-carrying boxes make good doll's houses because the inner dividers for the bottles can be easily transformed into room dividers. However, four smaller boxes fitted together in a square are even better. It is easier for the child to play if the front is open.

## What you can do

• Paper the walls with self-adhesive drawer-lining paper.
• Use matchboxes for kitchen cupboards, beds and other furniture.
• Draw on windows.
• Make curtains and bedcovers from scraps of fabric.
• Make food, dishes and even furniture from salt dough (see page 52).
• Make some pipe-cleaner people (see page 61) to live in the house.
• Details bring the house to life. Buy a doll's-house toilet and a bath (or make them from salt dough). Add blankets to beds.

A single, strong empty box can be adapted bit by bit to create another world.

## Making a camp

Constructing a camp is easy. If you have a garden with a washing line, just throw an old sheet over it. Pull out the sides and secure them with bricks and you have an instant tent. Inside the house, you could throw a sheet over a table or spread sheets between the back of the sofa and a couple of dining chairs.

Everyday objects can be converted into an indoor camp that sets the scene for hours of imaginative play.

## What you can do

• To make a quick camp, throw a large sheet over the kitchen table, or even over a washing line, and then weight down the edges with bricks.

• Clear out the bottom of a cupboard, but make sure the child can open the door from the inside.

• Hang a curtain or a sheet in front a lower bunk bed.

• Camps need cushions and perhaps a cardboard box for a treasure chest. Prepare an indoor picnic to make the camp very special.

• A camp can be a place for many forms of imaginative play: a special shop, a place to listen to tapes or to tell stories, or somewhere to do 'secret work'.

## Dressing-up box

Most children love dressing up. Sometimes they dress up to play the game, and this is almost always the case when they are with other children. But when children are by themselves they may just like to wear the costume.

## What you can do

• Small children find wrap-around cloaks and pull-on skirts with elastic waists easier to put on. If fastenings are needed, choose velcro.

• A perfectly acceptable cat can be made by adding ears to a black wool hat and a tail to a pair of black trousers. Paint on whiskers with face paints.

• Jumble sales and charity shops are a great source for mix-and-match dressing-up outfits. Children will love oversized shoes and waistcoats, gold dancing slippers, feather boas, and anything wih sequins, satin or fake fur.

## Knights of old

Young knights can safely have fun fighting battles with cannon balls (balls of scrunched-up newspaper) rather than swords. A bucket of burning coals (polystyrene packaging dipped in red or black poster paint) would be great to pour on invaders. To make a castle, you need at least four sturdy cartons from the supermarket or wine merchant. You

# What the child learns

● Encourages a child to amuse herself in make-believe.

● Helps your child play with other children.

● Stimulates imagination and planning.

● Promotes story-telling, self-expression and communication skills.

**Most children enjoy play-fighting with their own cardboard weaponry, painted in 'team' colours.**

can either open these up to make a folding castle or pile them up to make a barrier for the knights to hide behind. To make a folding castle, open out the top and bottom of each box and cut down one corner so you have a single sheet of cardboard. Cut the flaps from the top, but leave the bottom flaps – they improve stability. Draw the outline of the stones on to the card. Stick the sections of card together with parcel tape. Make battlements from thinner card and glue in place. The wall can be placed around a chair or sofa, or even his bed. For improved stability, secure it at intervals to the furniture or put some weights on the flaps. Make sure he can get in and out.

## What you can do
• Make safe swords from rolled-up sheets of newspaper.
• Make a shield from an old cereal package. Cut out the top and bottom of the box and stick these together to make the handle. Now cut out the front and back of the package and draw the outline of a shield on both pieces and cut out the shape. Make two slits in the middle of one piece of card, pass the handle through these slits and staple. Decorate the other piece to form the front of the shield. Glue together.
• Make simple armour from two pieces of card joined at the shoulder with ribbon. Just cut out a curve for the neck and the arms. Paint it grey or silver and then add an emblem of your child's choice on the front.

# music, movement and drama

# Physical play

Children have to let off steam every day. If you try to stop them, they will fidget and become restless and irritable. When you free them from constraints, they burst with boundless energy.

All children need regular periods of physical exertion, preferably with other children.

## It is in their nature

Most young animals play: they chase, wrestle, pounce and gambol. Human children are no exception. If you confine a healthy young child for more than an hour or two, her restlessness may become almost uncontainable. The fact that all young animals do this tells us that something important is happening here. Physiologists suggest that the sudden bursts of activity followed by stops and slower activities – the pattern of activity of children playing tag or kittens chasing and wrestling – is the ideal way of encouraging the proper development of muscles, bones and breathing.

## Space too

If you stop animals playing in this way, for example by raising them without frequent ready access to playmates, they will never really acquire spatial learning skills. They will take much longer to solve mazes, and will do badly in tests in which food is hidden in lots of different places. Compared to those who play normally and regularly with others, they will have a much lower attention span. It does not appear to take much rough and tumble to avoid these problems altogether. A short period of physical play every day seems to be enough.

Of course humans could be quite different, but why take chances? Time spent racing about is good fun, and recent research suggests that if children have a good race about between lessons there are fewer discipline problems in the classroom and children settle down to work better.

## Moving together

It is hard to keep moving when you are by yourself. Whatever our age, we are more likely to run, dance and chase about when we are with other people. If we want children to develop in the natural way and fulfil their potential, they need to spend time with other children and they need to be able to play freely as well as formally. Make regular opportunities for informal get-togethers with other children.

## What you can do

• Make opportunities for physical activity. Put on some music and dance together with your child.
• Go for a run together, play chasing games and have races. However you do it, make sure she has at least one period of strenuous physical activity daily.
• Make clearing-up a game. Put on some music and race to get everything picked up before it stops.
• Help her to learn to balance. Climbing helps, so does holding her hand while she walks on walls.
• Encourage her to catch and throw. Bean bags and balls of newspaper are safest indoors and are much easier than balls for young children to handle.
• Encourage her to copy your movements and be aware of her own body by playing games that demand specific movements.
• Let her jump off the bottom step, bounce on the bed and swing on a rope.

# Talent spotter

★ **Does your child move with more grace and precision than her peers? Does she run faster and jump higher?**

★ **Does she enjoy following your example by participating in physical activities?**

★ **Is she agile in her movements?**

★ **Are her skills with a ball well advanced (see the Development Charts, pages 20–31)?**

★ **Does she love physical activity?**

Encourage your child to let off steam with her playmates.

# Physical activity in all weathers

The easiest way to get children moving is to invite round a group of friends to play, or to play a chasing game in the garden. But what do you do when there is just the two of you and it is wet outside?

Bad weather need not stop children exercising and letting off steam.

## Indoor play equipment

Indoor play equipment can encourage physical activity when playing outside is not possible for some reason. However, for most of us there is simply not enough space to accommodate large items. With ingenuity, however, you can create space-saving alternatives that provide physical fun and games whatever the weather outside.

## What you can do

• Fix a sturdy hook into the ceiling, attaching it securely to a beam or joist. You can then attach a monkey swing or a long rope ladder for him to play on. A monkey swing is easier for a child to climb on to than a conventional swing. You can remove the swing or ladder when it is not in use.
• Rope ladders are great for climbing. Your child can climb to the top or just go up a couple of steps and swing. Put cushions underneath for softer landings.
• Bunk beds make good indoor climbing frames. Check whether it is possible to attach a slide safely.

• Always supervise your child when she is playing on equipment of any kind – whether purpose-made or improvised.

## Jumping off the stairs

Most children enjoy jumping off the stairs. Just put a pile of cushions at the bottom of the stairs for safe landings and make sure that your child does not try to jump down too many steps at a time. If she is prone to showing off – especially if there are friends around to show off to – it might be safer to jump off the sofa.

### What you can do

• Bouncing on an old chair or on a double bed is great fun.
• You can make an obstacle course that involves jumping down the stairs, walking on a line, crawling under a blanket and behind the sofa.

## Braving the weather

Encourage your child to enjoy the outdoors whatever the weather. Provided you are both properly dressed for the conditions, you can have fun playing outside in all kinds of weather. Stamping in puddles is always a great favourite with children and providing it is not raining too hard and you have the right clothes, you do not even need to wait for the rain to stop. Just put on your wet weather gear and boots and go out in search of the biggest puddles you can find in which to paddle and splash. Your laughter will reassure your child that it is okay to get wet.

All sorts of weather conditions can offer opportunites for games and fun.

### What you can do

• On windy days go out with flapping clothes and pretend you are being blown away. If you can, find a windy hill to climb for even more fun.
• Run around the block, jump up and down on the spot, and turn windmills.
• On snowy days go out and play snowballs or slide down the hill on a plastic bag. Make muddy, wet or snowy footprints.

Using paper plates as stepping stones is good balancing practice.

## Fun in the Snow

Waking up to the first snow of the year is always exciting. Even before the curtains are opened, there is often a quality of light and sound that tells you the snow is there.

### What you can do

• Encourage your child to fall over in the snow, making an imprint of his body.
• Show him how to make snowballs and throw them at a wall. Enjoy the splat!
• Build a snowman. A simple snowman just needs a carrot nose, some pebble eyes, a hat and a scarf and he is finished.

## Avoiding Sharks

It is hard to learn to balance if you do not practise. Use your imagination to make opportunities for practising around the house. Avoiding Sharks is a game my children enjoyed. Distribute paper plates across the room. The plates are stepping stones and the floor is water infested with sharks. The object is to get from one side to the other without stepping in the water. Older children can play this outside using bricks or flowerpots as islands.

### What you can do

• Walking the line. Lay a ribbon on the floor and fix it in place with masking tape. Ask your child to walk along the ribbon without falling off.
• Furniture hopping is another good indoor game. See if your child can get from one part of the room to another without touching the floor.

# What the child learns

● To enjoy physical activity. A child who has an active childhood is more likely to become an active adult.

● To laugh and play together with other children.

● Not to be worried about getting wet or dirty.

● To become confident about moving. To balance from one foot to the other and balance and move at the same time.

# Getting physical

Toddlers and young children are too young for formal sports or dancing lessons, but they can gain a great deal from 'pre' sports and dancing games. Such activities help your child to become aerobically fit and well co-ordinated.

## Just like me

Children need to become aware of their bodies and how they move through space. They need to know how to position themselves to get through gaps and to judge whether they are likely to knock something over as they walk past. Games in which children copy movements, such as Simon Says, help with this awareness, as does racing around the garden on a bike.

## What you can do

• To play Simon Says, 'Simon' must give instructions. If the prompter says 'Simon says put your hands on your head', you must do so. If he says 'Put your hands on your head', you do not. The child must only do what 'Simon says'. You can take it in turns to be Simon.
• Who can do the silliest walk? And can you copy it?
• Play the Hokey Cokey. Put your left leg in (forward) and your left leg out (back). Do this twice. Put your left leg in and shake it all about. Then you turn about and do the same with your right leg. You can make your own variations with movements of different parts of the body.

Games like Simon Says encourage awareness and co-ordination.

• Set out a line of flowerpots in the garden and let him do the slalom on his bike.
• Use a few handfuls of sand to mark out a road system in the garden – let him follow the road on his bike. Just rake in or sweep up the sand after he has finished.

## Into the mouth

Children find it easier to throw something they can grip, such as a beanbag or a scrunched-up ball of newspaper. Paint a big red open mouth on an old sheet with emulsion paint. His task is to throw scrunched-up balls of newspaper into the mouth, collect the balls and try again.

### What you can do
• Substitute a box for the mouth and use beanbags or balls instead of paper.
• Make skittles from old plastic bottles and roll balls to knock them over.
• Sit some distance apart and roll a small ball back and forth between you.
• Encourage him to throw a ball or beanbag for you to catch.
• Play catch with a beach ball and, as he becomes more skilled, reduce the size of the ball and move further away.
• Once he can stand on one leg, he will enjoy kicking a ball.
• Teach him how to hit a ball with a bat or a racquet.

## Obstacle courses

This is an all-time favourite for the under-fives, and especially good when a child needs cheering up. Be warned, though, if you have a gang of children, playing it can get a bit out of hand.

### What you can do
• Walk the plank. Put a builder's plank of wood (or a couple of very strong and sturdy wooden shelves) between two bricks and let the child walk the plank and jump off the end.

Playing catch will develop hand–eye co-ordination.

## Outdoor equipment

When everyone had large families and children played in the street or fields, outdoor equipment was unnecessary. Everything a child had to learn about moving through space could be learned by playing with other children. Now that many children spend a lot of their early childhood playing indoors, often by themselves, play equipment is much more important. If you have not got the space or the means to provide equipment at home, try to give your child access to an adventure playground in your local park.

## What you can do
• Give your child a 'sit-and-ride' bike to move around the garden.
• Provide a monkey swing or rope ladder to improve balance.
• Give your child access to a climbing frame or a slide to help him to improve his balance.
• Have a good supply of bats and balls of different sizes.

## Wet and wild
On a fine day there is nothing like a paddling pool, a garden sprinkler or chasing the child around the garden with a hose to encourage exuberant activity. Keep the hose pressure low and use an attachment that gives a spray. Never leave a child alone near water. Remember children can drown in a very shallow pool.

## What you can do
• Invite a friend or two along – they will race and chase and laugh together.
• On a cooler day, a chasing game with a threat of tickling can replace the water.
• If it is too cold for getting wet, float sail boats or lollypop sticks in the paddling pool.

# What the child learns

● To be aware of how his body moves.

● To observe and imitate movements.

● To enjoy being physically active and move with grace.

● To laugh and play with others.

● To balance.

● To propel things through space.

If you don't have a garden yourself, take your child to a local park or playground.

# Imaginative play

When we think about imaginative games, we usually think of a child dressed in a costume pretending to be someone else. But children do not always act out a role, and there are many ways in which they exercise their imagination.

## Three ways to pretend

Sometimes children pretend they are doing something, such as cooking in their toy kitchen. Sometimes they pretend to be someone else – perhaps Mummy or Daddy, an animal or a cartoon character.

**Children will enact an entire drama with the help of a few basic props that metamorphose in imaginative play.**

This type of pretending is like a play in which they act out a part. At other times their games of pretence are much more like telling a story in actions, or actions with words.

Children use their toys to create worlds in which they move their toy figures around, going on journeys, having adventures and speaking for their people. The child is the author and director of the play rather than an actor in it. Actors need costumes and child-sized props; a storyteller and director needs a cast of tiny characters and props for them.

## Traditional boys' worlds

A boys' world usually entails the movement of toys around a large play space. Train sets and miniature cars are the obvious examples.

Traditionally these toys did not have people the child spoke for, and young players made noises rather than spoke as they moved them. Cars went 'brumm', fire engines 'ee-ar, ee-ar' – and they still do. Some boys' worlds do have people – armies of soldiers or aliens from other planets, but they do not stand around and have a chat.

## Girls' worlds

Classic girls' worlds, such as dolls' houses, were the home of a family of little people. The child could play with the house by moving the pieces about and rearranging the layout, or the house could form the backdrop to a domestic game in which the dolls interacted and the child spoke on their behalf.

## Modern unisex worlds

When families were larger, and there was not much money for toys, most children developed story-telling skills by playing with older children. The increasing variety of books, television and videos have become part of the life of young children and the growth in 'little world' toys have paralleled this. There are farms and garages, schools and fire stations, alien space stations and fairytale castles. These are often unisex for two- to three-year-olds, but are sex-stereotyped for four- to six-year-olds.

## What you can do

• Read her stories, let her watch videos with you and expose her to all the different ways of story-telling.
• Provide her with the right toys. Long before she can hold a story in mind it can be drawn forward by the props she uses. A two-year-old cannot easily remember all the details she needs to play at cooking dinner, but if she has a toy kitchen she will be able to play the game with ease.
• Encourage boys to use language as they play and girls to use space, by providing toys such as cars full of little people that offer both opportunities.
• Do something special and talk about it when you get home. Provide the opportunity to play through experiences.

# Talent spotter

★ Does she prefer imaginative stories to factual books?

★ By the age of three, does a story soothe her when she is feeling sad?

★ By the age of four, is she starting to make up stories? Are her excuses wild and wonderful?

★ By four and a half, does she enact recent outings and experiences in her pretend games?

★ Can she play without someone else organizing the activity? When she is with other children, does she organize their pretend games?

★ By the age of four, does she incorporate pretend activities into more practical games such as building or bike-riding?

★ Does she overcome shyness by pretending to be someone else?

★ By the age of four, can she imitate actions and sounds?

★ Is she more graceful than other children of her age?

# Recreating experiences

Early games of make-believe recreate common daily experiences, such as cooking dinner or going to the shops. Older children are able to play through recent outings and experiences and retell fictional stories, but only if you provide the right props.

## In the kitchen

Cooking is one of the few household tasks that families carry out every day. So we should not be surprised that toy kitchens are among the most-used toys, and pretending to cook is perhaps the most popular pretend activity for two- to three-year-olds. Two-year-olds need to be realistic at this age. You may find that a couple of small real saucepans and a small frying pan elicit more play than toy pans with faces on them.

## What you can do

• A toy kitchen will provide opportunities for stimulating play for all young children. Your child will need a stove and a sink and perhaps a microwave if you use one.
• A small table and some play crockery and cutlery, extend the game. Add extra pans and some salt dough or papier mâché food to give to her teddies.
• Let her help you do some real cooking or food preparation. She could perhaps make sandwiches for a picnic.

## What the child learns

● To tell the story of her daily life. To remember and recount her daily experiences to herself and to you.

● To think things through, and to use language to express memories, emotions and feelings.

● To remember what happened last time she did something. To be watchful of details next time she is out.

● Toy money encourages counting; kitchen scales help her to understand concepts such as heavy and light.

● A camp isolates the child from distractions, useful for a child who finds it difficult to maintain concentration.

● To talk about things she can no longer see.

Pretending to be someone else helps a child to imagine how it must feel to be someone else.

## Holiday time

Once you get home from holiday, it is difficult for the child to remember what happened because the props she relies on to jog her memory are no longer present. She finds it difficult because her memories are mainly pictures. Help her to remember by recreating some of her experiences.

### What you can do

• If you stayed at a hotel, recreate the front desk, including a place for keys. Have another desk with a stamp (from a stationery shop) to stamp passports. Other office equipment will also be useful.
• Create a café with a table in the garden, an umbrella and some plates of pretend or real food.
• Use a few brochures, a phone and some tickets to make a travel agent.

• Tell the story of the holiday. Remind her of the details. Look at the photographs and discuss what happened on the day they were taken.

## Shopping

You can make play shops of all kinds. For example, the boxes you use for cardboard constructions can be used for a food shop. Collect the family shoes to make a shoe shop, cut out paper fish for a fish shop, or simply use the fruit and vegetables you have in your kitchen for a greengrocer's. It just needs a little bit of imagination.

### What you can do

• All shops need a till and some money. The small change from foreign trips or the change you have in your purse is better than pretend money.

## Indoor dens

Most young children love dens. Make a simple indoor den by putting up a tent or throwing a sheet over a large table. Provide a cushion for her to sit on and a few toys. She will probably play happily in this special place for quite a while.

### What you can do

• You can buy play houses and play tents. In the summer you can pitch a small tent in the garden.
• A fishing rod and a rucksack are ideal props for an expedition – even if it is only as far as the front door.

## Roads and other layouts

Preschool toy shops abound with dolls' houses, garages, farms and train sets but they are also quite simple to make.

### What you can do

• To make a road system, cut lengths of card, draw line markings and fix the strips together with adhesive tape to form varying lengths of road. Add to the interest in the form of crossroads, bends and intersections.
• A piece of hardboard makes a firm base for a farm or town. Add papier mâché hills, sandpaper roads and a little mirror for a pond.
• Lollipop people are wonderfully simple to make: just draw faces on the ends of lollipop sticks. They work as they are, or you could add some straw or string hair or tie on an apron.

A simple road system will help your child recount car journeys.

• A set of scales is an essential part of the fun if there is anything she could weigh.
• If you normally pay by credit card, can you make a card machine?
• Keep old receipts so she can hand them to her customers.
• For a shoe shop, she needs a mirror and something to measure shoe sizes. Line up the dining room chairs for the customers to sit on.
• Provide a few bags.
• Think of the finishing touches that will really bring the shop to life – for example, make an open and closed sign.

# Little worlds

A child who is exposed to stories, whether through books, TV or videos, is likely to want to create her own. Whether it is a simple toy car or an elaborate village, a favourite doll or a cupboard full of stuffed animals, the props for creating 'little worlds' are among the most popular toys.

## Dolls

Fifty years ago most girls had a baby doll and if they were lucky a doll's carriage and a pretend baby bottle. Today fashion dolls have largely replaced baby dolls, but they probably serve much the same purpose: they help girls to understand what it is to be a woman. Young children are establishing their gender identity, learning that they are, were and always will be female. Although feeling you are a woman is separate from acting in the way women are expected to act, children use sex role stereotypes to aid them in the learning process.

Because children are not subtle, the roles they use are not subtle. When women were caregivers and homemakers, the role they latched on to was looking after babies. Now women's roles are less distinct, they latch on to the glamour of fashion dolls to provide that stereotyped role. If she is growing up in an egalitarian environment, and your family has the same expectations for boys and girls, men and women, she will learn that gender identity need not be restrictive.

Children will play through their everyday experiences with their dolls.

### What you can do

• This is one area where you probably need to forget your prejudices and give your child her heart's desire. If her friends have fashion dolls she is unlikely to play with a baby doll.

Your child may not have visited a farm but will still enjoy playing with animals.

## What the child learns

● To use their imagination; sit still, pay attention and complete a task from start to finish.

● That those who enjoy playing her games are like her.

● That gender is a part of her sense of self.

• If you want your daughter to see that women can be more than fashion plates give her a positive idea of women's roles and expectations. Encourage activities that show women are not just pretty clothes. Do not fall into the trap of buying her fashion doll a gym kit rather than engaging in physical activities. Let her go running with you, go for long walks together, ride bikes, go skating or take her to a children's gym session.

• Take care not to reinforce the ideal of the impossible body shape of many fashion dolls.

## On the farm

You can buy a ready-made farm, or you can buy some little plastic animals and make a farmyard from cartons and boxes. Cows and sheep need a field, ducks need a pond and pigs need a sty. Barns and tractors are interesting extras but fences can be a little frustrating for very young children.

### What you can do

• The easiest way to make a toy farm is to buy two pieces of hardboard or the thinnest piece of MDF board. Suppliers will usually cut them to the right size for you. Join the pieces with thick tape. Having the board in two halves makes it easier to store away. Now paint on fields, roads and a farmyard. Stick a mirror tile on one board to make the duck pond. You can then make buildings and barns from boxes and cartons and buy some farm animals. Children often like to have families of animals – so look out for calves and lambs, too.

• For most city children a farm is another version of the domestic scene rather than a representation of country life. Let her play her own game in her own way.
• Take your child to visit a real farm if you can, or read stories about farms. Children find it hard to play if they do not know the 'story'.

## At the garage

Getting fuel for the car is part of most children's everyday experience, so it is an easy game to reconstruct. You can make a toy garage, but unless you can find some miniature fuel pumps the bought version is usually better. Look for versions that combine car parking and fuel supplies.

### What you can do
• You can make a simple garage from a piece of card or board (as for a farm, above). Make fuel pumps from matchboxes. Treasury tags (available from stationery shops) make excellent nozzles for the pumps.
• A garage can be part of a more elaborate road layout.

## A trip on the train

Instead of talking, children play through their everyday experiences. Taking your child on an outing to create the experiences for their imaginative play does not have to be elaborate to fuel these stories. It just has to be different.

### What you can do
• The first thing to do is to plan the trip. Talk about trains. Tell your child about buying the ticket, about the platform and about getting on the train. Go down and look at the station.

Small children love playing with scaled-down versions of reality.

• Take her on a trip. It does not need to be far. Two stops on a suburban train is exciting, a three-hour train journey probably is not!
• Look for little details that will make the recreation of the trip special. Perhaps you could keep your ticket stubs and a copy of the timetable leaflet to use later on.
• When you get home sit with her and talk about your day.
• Provide the props for her to play with while the experience is still fresh in her mind: a line of chairs for her soft toys to sit on, some tickets and a hat so she can be the ticket-collector and rip up the old tickets.

# Dressing up

Drama involves dressing up and pretending to be someone else, but when he first puts on his father's old hat your child is just wearing a costume, not playing a part.

Young children will often identify with extreme gender stereotypes.

## Being themselves

By the time a child reaches his second birthday, he is able to refer to himself as 'me' or 'my', and he will recognize himself in the mirror or in family photographs. But, although he knows 'me', he does not yet understand that his thoughts and feelings are separate from everyone else's. When he puts on a police hat, there is no reason why he should think he is a police officer; he just likes wearing the hat. In their early years, children do not clearly separate reality and pretence. They are uncertain whether stories are true or how memories of real experiences and the stories they are told differ from each other.

## Imitating actions

Children start imitating the things we do soon after birth and by the time he is ten months he may imitate drinking by bringing a cup to his mouth as if he was going to drink. He is probably using an action as a word – like lifting his arms when he wants to say 'pick me up'. In fact, a lot of early make-believe games are like talking or thinking things through. Children do not join in role-play games until after their second birthday. Up to the age of four, there is no indication that he separates being someone else from pretending to be someone else. The first indication he can do this is usually between the ages of four and five. At this age he may say things like 'Pretend that I am the Daddy and you are the baby', showing that he understands the difference between playing a role and being that person.

Children vary a great deal in how much of their play is directed towards doing practical things and how much is involved in imaginative play. Some children spend much of their childhood being someone else, while others spend it drawing, constructing and racing around on bikes. You can encourage pretend play by reading plenty of stories – especially those that paint pictures in words and stretch his imagination.

## What you can do

• Make a collection of dressing-up clothes. Most girls enjoy glitzy and glamorous outfits; most boys prefer something altogether more masculine – hats, boots and cloaks. Charity shops are very good sources of original and different dressing-up clothes.
• Select the essential props – veils, jewels, cloaks, bags and phones.
• Put everything in a drawer or special box. Alternatively hang them on easily accessible coat hooks. Keep all elements of each outfit in a separate bag on the hook.
• He may need help putting on and taking off the outfit, but it is good practice for dressing and undressing.
• Adapt clothes to his needs. Some children hate things going over their heads, some have problems with buttons. Make necks wide and put the fastenings on the front where he can reach them. Velcro is the easiest fastener for the youngest children.

# Talent spotter

★ Does he seem to enter a world of his own?

★ Is dressing-up his favourite game?

★ Does he become engrossed in the character?

★ Does he put on a show?

★ Does he enjoy watching himself in the mirror?

★ When other children are playing, does he organize the game?

★ Does he play pretend games more than other children?

You can soon put together a collection of dressing-up clothes.

# Being someone else

Small children cannot organize complex thoughts or think about things in an abstract way. Your child has to act things out instead. When she dresses up and plays at doing the things adults do, she is able to think about the roles other people play in her life.

Even after children have learnt to distinguish pretence and reality, they still get engrossed in play-acting.

## Mothers and fathers

Parents are the central characters in a child's life, but children are not the only element of our lives; we go to work, we care for other children, we go out after she has gone to bed. She needs to work out that we do not share her thoughts, feelings and desires, and why her priorities are not always the same as ours. The only way she can gain insight into our world is to pretend to be us – which is what a child often does.

## What you can do

• Children need props that characterize you and your different roles – for example, glasses, a mobile phone, a briefcase, some high-heeled shoes.
• They need something that characterizes your special role within the household – for example, a paintbrush, some saucepans, a drill, a sewing machine.
• They need something to characterize your hobbies – for example, a gym bag, a fishing rod, a pretend pair of binoculars or a garden rake.

## Boys will be boys

Children learn their gender identity before they go to school. To learn what it is to be a man, a boy must distinguish the things men do from those that women do. This used to be straightforward but has become more difficult in recent years. Because the extremes are easier to distinguish, children latch on to these. No matter that his father is a gentle man who does domestic chores, if a child needs to see the distinction between a man and woman, the latest superhero will embody the essence of masculinity. Do not worry if your son does not play macho games. Some boys learn about gender identity in other ways.

**What you can do**
• Let him watch the antics of cartoon superheroes if he wants to.
• Make him an outfit so he can dress up as his favourite character. Cloaks and hats are useful. Cloaks are easy to make and, if you make the fastenings of Velcro, they are the easiest to put on and take off.
• The most popular prop for a superhero is something to zap the enemy (see Guns, page 96).

## Girls will be girls

Just as boys latch on to the macho images, girls often latch on to the extremes of femininity. The favourite outfits in their dressing-up box are usually glittery, glamorous and entirely unlike anything you would usually wear. However, there are always exceptions and some girls don't play these games. Do not worry if your daughter is a tomboy from the start; she will learn about her gender identity in other ways.

Boys often want to portray macho characters they have seen on TV.

**What you can do**
• She will want gold shoes, feather boas, sequined tops, satin dresses and lots of jewellery. You can buy glamorous outfits or seek out the components in charity shops and markets.
• Cut some of your old dresses down to size. It does not matter how wide they are, but obviously they are safer if she does not trip over the hem.
• Brides and princesses are always popular. As long as she has a veil, the dress does not need to be more elaborate than a cut-down white nightdress or petticoat.

Just because your child wants a gun does not mean he will play in a violent way.

## Guns

If you are fortunate enough to live in a social environment where all parents say no to toy guns, and none of your child's friends owns one, he may never mention them.

If his friends have or want guns, it will be harder to refuse. He will probably improvise by picking up sticks, pointing them and making firing noises. He may even build himself one with a construction kit.

### For and against

• There is no clear evidence that when children play with 'violent' toys, they act in more violent ways. It is how children play rather than what they play that is important. Gun games can be violent but so can football. A game of goodies and baddies can be co-operative and trusting. A board game can come to blows.

• Children spend less time playing with guns that are given to them than they spend thinking about forbidden guns.

• Children growing up in aggressive families and cultures are more likely to be aggressive themselves. A culture in which gun ownership is the norm is more likely to be a violent one. Children may be influenced to believe that having a gun is normal if all their toys have weapons.

Ultimately this is a matter of principle for you to decide. There is nothing wrong in standing your ground if this is important for you. Love combined with firm and fair rules is the main aim.

# What the child learns

● To see and understand you as a separate person.

● To see herself and her role in the family.

● To amuse herself.

● To become clearer about her gender identity and to understand differences between men and women.

● To spend time by herself.

# More than play-acting

Your child may have to have a light on because of the 'ghosts' under the bed but he also loves to run around with a sheet over his head shouting 'whoooooo' while you pretend to be afraid. Role-play has an important part to play in helping a child deal with fear and other issues.

## Ghosts and monsters

It is perfectly normal and sensible for small children to be afraid sometimes. Children are mainly afraid of losing you or of becoming separated from you. They are also afraid that something big might carry them away, and this was probably a realistic fear for our primitive ancestors. It is wise to be cautious, but it is not good to be so afraid that you cannot think or act sensibly. Children have to learn how to deal with their fears.

One of the most popular and successful treatments for phobias in adults is to think about that which frightens you most, while trying to remain happy and relaxed. This is what children who are afraid of ghosts are doing when they dress up in a sheet and play silly (and happy) games. They are coming to terms with their fears.

## What you can do

• If your child has a specific fear, look for suitable books that deal with the thing they are afraid of. Cuddle up and read them together so that he can feel safe while he thinks frightening thoughts.
• Draw pictures together of friendly monsters or make some out of play dough.

Children can often learn to deal with their fears through play-acting.

Play-acting does not need elaborate costumes.

## Being a ghost or a monster

Halloween is a good time to look for inspiration here. You may be able to buy old curtains in a local charity shop to make a ghost costume.

### What you can do

• Use a balloon with a wig to make an extra head.
• A net curtain dyed a lurid green with sections splattered with red would make a convincing monster costume.
• Use tights stuffed with pillowcases for extra arms and legs.
• Cotton wool dyed black and fixed to rubber bands could be used for hairy feet.

• Act scared when he dresses up as a ghost. If he laughs at your fear, he is learning to cope.
• Tell silly ghost stories, be afraid together and then laugh.
• Read plenty of traditional fairy tales. These have been honed over hundreds of years to combine frightening elements with the comfort of a happy or morally just ending.
• Coping does not always have to be fun. If a member of the family or a favourite pet dies, he will naturally be afraid that other people may die too. Sitting together sharing memories and tears is the natural response. As you cuddle up together, it is sadness rather than fear that brings the tears.

## Being an animal

Real animals do not say anything, but the animals in his books act as if they were human. So it is easy for a child to pretend to be a rabbit – there is nothing special he has to do or say except wear the rabbit ears, speak in a high voice and hop. Sometimes he may ask for some lettuce, and may like you to call him your 'special bunny' but often he just wants to wear the outfit.

### What you can do

• Stories help him to play animal roles as well as human ones.
• He may not need the full costume. Ears and a tail are often all that is necessary to turn him into the animal of his choice.
• If he does not have a costume, face paints may be enough to get him into the role. As we know from his drawings, the face is the most important part. Be sure to let him see his new face in the mirror.

# What the child learns

● How to cope when he feels afraid and how to control emotions.

● To imagine, to laugh and share fun.

● To come to terms with specific fears. Being someone else helps him understand himself. It also helps him to learn that other people are separate and different.

● To understand that everyone has their own feelings.

Dressing up for the sake of dressing up is often a game in itself.

## The vital ingredient

There is always something that turns a dressing-up outfit into the 'real thing' – the policeman's hat, the postman's sack, the fairy's wings, the bride's veil or the elephant's trunk. Sometimes all you need to provide for a successful game is this one vital ingredient.

### What you can do

• Ask your four-year-old to draw the person or activity he wants to be or do. Whatever he includes is what he thinks is important.
• Be observant. What would you want to include?

## Playing together

When a group of young children play dressing-up games, they rarely have a master plan. They do not dress to fit predetermined roles as older children would, but often dress up for the sake of dressing up, putting on whatever odd assortment of garments takes their fancy. The game is 'dressing up', which means putting on your finery and parading about.

### What you can do

• Fighting over the most favoured item in the dressing-up box is a common problem. It may be wise to take the item out of the box before his friends arrive.
• Keep something special in reserve. If one child has grabbed the gold lamé trousers or the Batman cape, bringing out a veil or a plastic shield may even things up.

# Interactive games

Children develop their interactive skills in the context of games. As they grow older, increasingly complex skills are needed, such as knowing how to mislead or deceive competitors. There are games that help children to learn how to do this too.

## The way we are

One person grows the grain, another person grinds it, and various people cook, wrap and sell it before it reaches our table as bread. Children have to learn to understand the complexities of human social organization, with its shared jobs and responsibilities and levels and types of interdependent relationships. Games, especially those that involve working in teams, help children learn to work together to achieve a specific end.

## Traditional games

Some of the games children play, such as traditional skipping games, have been in our culture for hundreds of years. We can be sure that the games children did not

Arch games, like Oranges and Lemons, are ideal for small children.

enjoy playing (or those that did not teach them something) have been weeded out long ago. Not all games are suitable for preschool children. Children under the age of six, for example, cannot weigh up the odds or cope with strategy so they play board games like ludo (where you have to decide which piece to move) without checking out the alternative moves. The game loses the element of skill and becomes one of chance. Games such as skipping may be too physically demanding, while games of skill such as marbles may need to be simplified.

## Choosing games

Because small children no longer play out on the street with older children, the first time they come into contact with a traditional game may be at a birthday party. Even here the professional entertainer is slowly taking over. This is in some ways a pity because children obviously gain more from playing together than from being entertained. The best games for younger children are ring games like Ring-o-Roses or arch games like Oranges and Lemons. By the time she is four, she can manage games that include an element of deception and games that need a little forward planning, such as Sardines (see page 102) or Musical Cushions (see page 103).

## What you can do

• Children need to practise playing together. Find opportunities for her to play with children her own age and also to join in with older children if possible.
• Activities like swimming are fine, but try to avoid filling all your child's social hours with scaled-down versions of adult activities. Children also need time for free play.

# Talent spotter

★ Does she seem to be aware of her body? Is she graceful and less clumsy than other children of her age? By the age of three can she copy movements? Does this skill continue to improve as she grows?

★ When playing in a group, does she seem more aware of other children's whereabouts than they are of hers?

★ Does she enjoy the company of other children and by the age of four does she play co-operatively?

★ By the age of four, does she easily grasp the rules of simple board games?

★ By the age of four, does she show signs of being able to plan the next move or develop a basic strategy?

★ By the age of five can she lose without sulking?

★ Has she always been more interested in people than she is in objects?

★ Are her social skills advanced (see the Development Charts, pages 20–31)? Can she put other children at their ease? Do other children want to play with her?

# Let's have a party!

Traditional party games are the ideal way to amuse a group of children. You will need to keep it simple for the youngest children, choosing games that are mainly an excuse for running around. Winners (or players) can get a small prize, but make sure that prizes are evenly distributed.

## Hiding games

In the classic game of Hide-and-Seek, one child covers his face while the others go off and hide. After a prearranged length of time – usually a count to 20 – he shouts 'Coming, ready or not!' and then goes in search of the other children.

## What the child learns

● To see other people's strategies and develop their own.

● To learn to be a loser as well as a winner.

● To have fun, share laughter and interact with a group.

● To anticipate what other people will do.

## What you can do

● In a more complex version, the seeker has to protect his base as well as find everyone else. If another child can get back to his base without been seen (or tagged) by the seeker, he avoids being seeker next. The person who is found or tagged first is the seeker next time.

● Sardines is a version of Hide-and-Seek in which everyone ends up hiding together. The children gather in one room while one child goes out of the room to hide. Those in the room count or sing a song before going off to find the hiding place. When they find it they climb in too. Soon everyone is packed as tight as sardines in a tin.

● Bug and Rug is a variation of Hide-and-Seek where, if you are found, you can run 'home'. If you can get there without being caught, you are safe. In other variations, you can run 'home' when it is safe before you are even spotted.

● You could also try variations where only one person hides and everyone else seeks.

## When the music stops

For Musical Cushions, have a cushion or pillow for each child. Arrange these in a line with a gap between each one. When the music stops each child finds a cushion and sits down. After a few turns, take away one cushion. When the music stops, the child who is left without a cushion to sit on is out of the game. Continue to remove a cushion at the end of each round until there is only one cushion left. The person who sits on it wins.

### What you can do
• This game can be played with dining chairs. Line them up so alternate chairs face in opposite directions.
• In Musical Hats, everyone has a silly hat instead of a cushion. They sit in a circle and pass hats in one direction. A hat is taken out each time; the one who is wearing the last hat when the music stops wins.
• In Hot Potato, the children sit in a circle and pass the potato around. The 'potato' can be an actual potato or a ball or similar-sized object. You need to pass it on before the music stops. The child left holding the potato is out.
• In Pass the Parcel, the parcel consists of many layers of wrapping, at the centre of which is the gift. The parcel is passed around the circle, and the child holding the parcel when the music stops unwraps one layer. If you like, you can put a tiny gift between each layer. The child who eventually reveals the gift wins it.

## Don't move!

Grandmother's Footsteps is a classic game with lots of variations. In the best-known version, one player – grandmother – sets up camp, usually against a tree or wall. The other players line up some distance away. Grandmother turns her back on the players who creep towards her while she is not looking. Grandmother can turn around without warning, and if she sees anyone moving they are out. The first person to tap Grandmother on the back wins and gets to play Grandmother next time.

Grandmother's Footsteps.

## What you can do

• Traffic Lights is a variation on Grandmother's Footsteps. One person is chosen to be the traffic light and stands out front with his back to the other children. He then shouts 'green light' and everyone creeps forward to try and touch the traffic light. From time to time the traffic light shouts 'red light' and spins around. Everyone must stand absolutely still. Anyone caught moving becomes the traffic light for the next game. The only difference in Grandmother's Footsteps is that 'Grandmother' does not give any warning of when she is going to turn round.

• Musical Statues is a simpler game. The children dance around until the music stops. Then, whatever position they are in, they must remain completely still. No tickling, but you can try to make people laugh to get them to move. If they move they are out and the music starts again. Those who are out have the fun of being checkers for the next round.

• Guardsmen is a more sophisticated version. It's great fun at a picnic in a wooded area where there are lots of hiding places, although you will need to supervise a group of young children. You need at least three players but it is best with a crowd. One child (the guardsman) covers his eyes and stands at his base while everyone else hides. The guardsman then marches up and down between two points. He can look straight ahead but must not move his head to the side. The other children have to get back to the base without being seen (or if there are few hiding places, without being seen to move). They can run and creep when his back is turned but must have a hiding place ready to dive into before he turns back at the end of his patrol.

**Many party games allow children to play together with few formalities.**

# Just fun

A child who knows how to have fun is truly creative. They may not win the glittering prizes but they certainly win the ones that matter – happiness, friendship and the feeling of a supportive network around them. Songs with actions, without winners or losers, are among the most successful party games.

## The big ship sails

*The big ship sails through the ally ally oh*
*The ally ally oh, the ally ally oh*
*The big ship sails through the ally ally oh*
*On the 19th of December.*

Everyone holds hands and makes a line. The tail of the line puts his arm against a wall and the head of the line comes under the arch he has made. When the last player goes through, the tail person is turned around with his arms crossed. Now the arch is made between the tail and the next player and the line goes around again. The line keeps going around until everyone is wound up and its time to unwind or start the game again.

Even the youngest child can join in Oranges and Lemons.

## Oranges and Lemons

Oranges and Lemons is another ancient arch game. Two people make an arch that everyone else skips through, one behind the other. They keep going round and around singing:

*Oranges and lemons say the bells of St Clement's,*
*You owe me five farthings, say the bells of St Martin's,*

*When will you pay me? say the bells of Old Bailey,*
*When I grow rich, say the bells of Shoreditch,*
*When will that be? say the bells of Stepney,*
*I'm sure I don't know, says the great bell of Bow.*

Then the arch catches and releases children as they sing:

*And here comes a candle to light you to bed*
*And here comes a chopper to chop off your head.*
*Chop, chop, chop …*

and with the final CHOP a child is caught. He then becomes part of the arch and the song is resumed until all the children have been caught.

**Make a game of ghosts more fun by providing some ghostly props.**

## Aya Aya Conga

This is a game played by adults at the end of a party, but it is also suitable for children. Just make a long line by holding on to the waist of the person in front. If small children find this difficult, just give them a rope to hold on to in a line. All they have to do is follow the line singing 'Aya Aya Conga', following the twists and turns made by the person at the head of the line. This is good played to music.

## Net-curtain ghosts

You will need some lengths of net curtain – charity shops are a good source. Put a piece over the head of each child and secure it in place with a headband. Let them run about shouting 'Whooooo', pretending to be ghosts.

### What you can do
• If you want to extend the theme, a joke shop will provide useful props.
• Make a wall from paper and cut a few slits so they can walk through it.

## The farmer's in the dell

*The farmer's in the dell, the farmer's in the dell*
*E, I, N, G, O, the farmer's in the dell*

This is a circle game in which a child who has been chosen to be the farmer stands in the middle while the others hold hands and dance around singing as they go. After the first verse they sing 'The farmer wants a wife' stopping after the 'E I N G O' for him to choose a wife from the circle. Other verses follow: 'the wife wants a child', 'the child wants a dog' and 'the dog wants a bone'. At the end of each verse, another child is

# What the child learns

**Many musical ring games started life as formal dances.**

● Having and sharing fun, anticipating, laughing, but most of all enjoying the company of other children, even those he does not know.

● To use simple strategies to get the most out of each game.

● Singing is always a good ice-breaker for groups of children who do not know each other well. Although everyone joins in, nobody has to do anything very difficult.

chosen from the circle. The final verse is 'we all pat the bone'. However, leave this out unless you are sure the bone will cope with being patted.

## What you can do
There are many variations on circle games:
• 'Ring-a-ring o Roses, A pocket full of posies, Atishoo, Atishoo we all fall down.' And everyone falls over.
• In Lucy Locket or Drop the Hanky the children sit in a circle. A child skips around the outside with a hanky. He drops it behind one child's back, who must then chase and catch him before he gets back to his place in the circle.

## What's the time Mr Wolf?
'One o'clock', 'two o'clock' and you are safe, but when the wolf says '12 o'clock DINNER TIME!' you have to run. Whoever he captures first is the wolf on the next go.

## What you can do
• There are many variations on tag, in which one child chases and attempts to catch the others. Once caught, they become the chaser. You can decree, for example, that it is safe off the ground or if you are touching wood.
• In Duck, Duck, Goose, the goose goes around touching everyone, saying 'duck-duck'. But when he says 'goose' it is time to run before he catches you.
• Sleeping Lions is an invaluable cool-down game when you think the children may be getting overexcited. The children lie on the floor and try to keep absolutely still. Anyone seen moving is out and becomes a checker. No touching or tickling is allowed, but you can try to make the sleeping lions laugh.

# Music, song and dance

Although some children start to play the violin at the age of two and take dancing lessons from three, most experts agree that more children give up music and dance because they started formal training too early. It is better to start late and continue.

## Introducing music

Let your children hear music, move to music and join in when you sing and play. But do not start music lessons before they are at school, unless you can give them time to sustain the activity. Even if you have that time, be careful to maintain a clear balance between his desire to play and your own desire for him to become a musician. Start him earlier only if you have the time and energy to practise with him every day, and the clear-sightedness to call a halt if his motivation starts to flag.

He does not need to start this early to become a world-class musician; he can wait until he is eight to ten years old. Learning to read is hard work; so is learning to play an instrument. Doing both at the same time does not leave the child much time for fun, relaxation or mastering social skills. It is best to let children master reading before they begin music. This does not mean that young children cannot enjoy musical activities. On the contrary, listening, playing percussion, dancing and singing are important to a young child.

## Singing a limited tune

Most children can only sing a limited range of notes, but they can hear a much larger range. Nursery songs use this small range and small children sing them more or less in tune. Let your child sing nursery songs with you for pure pleasure, then gradually help him to extend his range. Songs with actions help him remember the words and tune.

Playing a percussion instrument can help to develop a sense of rhythm.

## Moving to music

Most children move spontaneously to music and encouraging them to dance is not difficult. Expose your child to a variety of music from rock to classical ballet scores and encourage him to move in different ways. Let him sit on your knee or rest in your arms while you move to the music. Move up and down with the tones, slow and fast with the rhythm, soft and strong with the volume. In other words, teach him to listen and respond to all aspects of the sound.

## What you can do

• Expose children to music from an early age. Babies like to watch videos with music rather than spoken words; or turn down the sound on a favourite video and put on a disc. Try to pair the same pictures and music each time.
• Let your child know you like music.
• Dance with him in your arms and encourage him to move to music.
• Cuddle up and listen, let music soothe him when he is sad or tired.
• Jog him on your knee, jump up and down with him in your arms in time to music and let music be part of his natural exuberance.
• Action songs help a child to remember the words and the tune.
• Clap out the rhythm or tap it out on the table.
• Teach him simple songs and encourage him to join in.
• If you play an instrument, give him a drum or a jar full of beans to shake and join in while you practise.
• Find a pre-dancing class where children are encouraged to move to music in an informal way.

# Talent spotter

★ Does musical ability and appreciation run in your family?

★ Since babyhood has he always responded to music?

★ Does music soothe him when he is sad?

★ Does he sing and move to music when he is happy?

★ Does he have a natural sense of rhythm?

★ By the age of three, can he clap or move in time to music?

★ Can he sing better than most children of his age?

★ Does he try to join in when another person is playing music?

# Let the children sing

The ability to excel at making music seems to run in families, but this does not mean that members of 'unmusical' families cannot learn to play an instrument or sing in tune. Children sing spontaneously although they are not always very tuneful.

Blowing out candles helps to develop the breath control needed to play brass and wind instruments.

## Learning to listen

Small children often have trouble concentrating for more than a few minutes, so the first steps in music are mostly about learning to listen and notice the difference between similar sounds and to realize how a certain pattern of sound can express an emotion or build a picture.

## What you can do

• Shake a package of rice and a package of split peas. Can your child tell the difference? Now do it behind her back. Can she still tell which is which? You can also try using a wooden spoon, then a metal spoon to hit a saucepan lid.
• Practise saying 'Cooee' (*coo* is high and *ee* is lower). Try shouting it, humming it, whistling it or whispering it and get her to copy you.
• Listen to music and sing together.
• Sing, speak, shout or play recordings of pairs of different sounds. Some of the sound-pairs should be the same, others should be different. If the sounds are the same, the child shouts SNAP.

# What the child learns

● To enjoy simple music-making and to listen.

● To match a pattern of breathing to an activity. To sustain a breath so that he can sing and play long notes.

● To be aware of sounds and understand that music can express emotions and feelings or 'paint a picture'.

● To understand that music is a social activity that makes us feel close and included in the social group.

● Playing percussion allows the child to feel in control.

● To appreciate and respond to rhythm.

## Breath control

Singing requires good breath control, and so does playing wind and brass instruments. Good breath control also helps us to maintain physical activity and promotes the supply of oxygen to the brain. It is always worth teaching a child to fit breathing to the activity.

**What you can do**
• Teach your child to blow out candles. Then teach him to bend the flame by blowing gently without blowing it out.
• See how long he can hold a note. Can he hold his breath for a count of five?
• Practise blowing paint with a straw and using a straw for drinking.
• Blow bubbles.
• Encourage your child to run fast, then jog, then walk. Breathing patterns change with the level of effort involved.

## Nursery rhymes and songs

Children find it easier to remember rhymes and songs than stories. The pattern and rhythm helps them recall more complex sentences and words than they could otherwise manage. Rhythm helps them hear the sounds that make up words and can help a child overcome reading problems.

**What you can do**
• Teach your child nursery rhymes and songs. If you cannot sing in tune, back up your rendition with more tuneful tapes.
• Sing lullabies when he is sleepy, and play singing games when he is happy.
• Listen to music together. Listen to silence. Listen to the birds singing.

## Musical stories

This is a game that can be played in two ways. The first is to use music as part of your story-telling to replace a character or to predict when a character is about to appear in a story. Use a particular tune as a sort of flourish that you put in each time the hero appears or as a warning, for example, before the wolf gobbles up Grandma. You can also use it to embellish a story by giving each child a tune to sing or a noise to make whenever their character appears. This can lead to great hilarity.

### What you can do

• Action songs help children fit words and music together and help small children anticipate the next notes.
• Singing together is the best way to teach a child that music is to be enjoyed and shared.

## Jam-jar symphony

Find half a dozen glass tumblers, jam jars or glass bottles. Put different amounts of water into each, so some are almost empty and others are almost full. Show your child how to tap each glass gently with a wooden spoon or the end of a paintbrush to make a note.

### What you can do

• Change the amount of water to change the note of the jar.
• Experiment with jars of different shapes to make different sounds.
• Let your child 'tune' his jar by allowing him to pour in extra water or pour some water out.

Young children love to join in with action songs.

# Let the children dance

Not all young children can sing in tune. In fact, some are horribly tuneless. But almost all children can learn to move rhythmically to music and express themselves through that movement. They will also learn to appreciate the tempo allowed by various kinds of music.

## Silly walks and graceful glides

Can he hop like a rabbit, glide like a swan, or creep like a cat stalking a bird? Can he put out his arms and fly to a soaring melody? If you are unsure where to find musical inspiration, film soundtracks are a good starting place. Movement is a small child's first means of expression. He combines it with words, and if encouraged will combine it with music.

## What you can do

• Look out for books of children's action songs and rhymes, or make up your own actions to accompany songs you know.
• Ballet music is specifically written to accompany and inspire dance. You do not need to know the choreographer's interpretation to recognize when the dance movement changes. Let your child move in any way he wants.

## Up and down

Does your child understand that notes rise and fall? Can he hear them going up and down? Does he understand that some notes are short and others sustained? You can help him learn by playing this simple game.

Encourage your child to dance to her favourite songs.

## What you can do

• Stand at the bottom of the stairs or the garden steps. Play or sing two notes, one after the other. If the notes rise, he steps up. If they fall he steps down. You will need to make this very obvious at first and do it together the first few times.

• Stand with hands together and open them slowly while a note is sustained. The further apart the hands are the longer the note.

## Dance till you drop

You may find there is a time, an hour or so before bedtime, when young children no longer seem to have the attention or energy for mentally challenging activities. It may be too early for his bath and he is too restless for his story. This is the ideal time to put on music and have a bedtime bop. This releases pent-up energy that otherwise leads to fidgeting, which can disturb the child's concentration.

## What you can do

• If your child is reluctant to dance, just let him run about.

• Dance with him.

• Let him dance by putting his feet on your feet.

• Try a little line dancing or carry him in your arms and do a tango.

## Can I dance on your feet?

This is a game that produces laughter and high spirits, and also teaches the child to follow and fit in with the movements of others.

## What you can do

• Put on a fairly slow tune.

• The child takes off her shoes and puts one foot on top of each of your feet and you hold her in place.

• In theory, then you dance. In practice, it will probably take some time to learn how to move together. Start by walking up and down in one direction first, then try taking steps from side to side.

**Dancing on an adult's feet encourages an appreciation of movement from an early age.**

Show your child how to clap in time to music.

# What the child learns

● To use his body to interpret music and express himself.

● To think about different sorts of music.

● That music is made up of notes that change in pitch and duration.

● To listen carefully and pay attention to detail.

● To recognize the beat, but mostly to have fun.

● To breathe and move in time with the beat.

## Clearing-up music

This is a useful technique I learned when I was doing some research in a Japanese preschool. When it was time to clear up, the school put on the special clearing-up music. All the children sprang into action, racing to get everything put away in the cupboards before the music stopped.

**What you can do**
• Choose special music to remind children that it is time to think of finishing up an activity. Do not just say 'five minutes', say 'here is the five-minute music'.
• Have a special cuddle tune that you put on before bedtime, a soothing song before sleep, or music to dance to before settling down.

## I got rhythm

Some children have a natural sense of rhythm. When they hear the beat they automatically move in time. Other children find it much harder to move with the rhythm of the music.

**What you can do**
• Put your child on your knee and jog him up and down in time to the music.
• Clap together in time to the music.
• Gently pat his back in time to the music.
• Hold him in your arms and bounce up and down in time to the music.
• Give him drumsticks (or a couple of wooden spoons) to 'play' the arm of the sofa.
• Give him a drum, a tambourine or a shaker to play along with the music.

# words and numbers

# Thinking creatively

It is a child's questions that tell us she has been trying to work something out. It is not solving the problem that makes her creative; it is knowing that there are questions she should be asking.

Talking to your child about the day's events may help to boost his memory.

## Concentrating

The younger she is the harder she finds it to concentrate. Adults cope with distraction by 'parking' their thoughts for a few minutes while attending to something else, but children under the age of six cannot do this – if distracted for more than a moment or two they forget what it was they were thinking before. The younger they are, the more likely this is to happen. This means that, to be a creative thinker, a child needs thinking time without distractions. Make a time each day when you turn off the television and radio and put extra toys away so that she can really learn to concentrate on a single task.

## Settling down

Children like a quiet place to do their 'work' and will play happily as long as they can look up and see you close by. If she has to worry about where you are, she will be distracted. Keep in view and when you are leaving the room let her know. She will also be distracted if she has to worry about making a mess or getting her clothes dirty. Mess is not a problem if you are prepared for it. Set aside a time each day for messy play and use plastic sheets and aprons to protect your furniture and her clothes.

## Helping her to remember

Adults put experiences into words and use those words as memory cues. Children do not do this spontaneously. The cues they need to retrieve memories are sounds, sights and smells. Unless you talk about the dog that jumped into the pond, she will only remember it when she goes back to the park. Quiet chats about the day's events help her to learn to think about things that happened somewhere else.

## Understanding jokes

Children start to tell jokes before they understand why they are funny. To see the funny side, you have to hold the literal meaning of the joke and the silly meaning in mind at the same time, or anticipate one meaning while hearing another. For the single-track mind of a young child, this is impossible. Ask a four-year-old for a variation on her favourite joke and she will tell you something that is not funny. By the age of seven she can hold two ideas in mind, so she understands why something is funny.

## What you can do

• Provide her with the right tools: factual books, plenty of conversation and explanations, interactive games and opportunities to experiment.
• Encourage her to look for explanations – even if they are wrong.
• Challenge her by playing games that stretch her memory and that require attention and concentration.
• Enjoy her cleverness. Let her know you are proud of her, but do not let her think that you only love her because she is clever.
• Try not to push her into new activities. Those who spend their lives learning do so because it gives them pleasure.

# Talent spotter

★ Since toddlerhood has she been able to amuse herself?

★ Has she always wanted to work out for herself how things fitted or what they did, before she asked for help?

★ Compared with other children of her age, are her social skills good? Is she aware of other people's actions? Does she tell stories in pretend play?

★ Did she use words and actions to express herself before she was ten months old? Was her language development precocious?

★ Compared with children of the same age does she have good concentration levels?

★ Will she sit quietly and watch an insect entering a flower or water running down the windowpane?

★ Has she always asked questions?

★ Does she spontaneously look for explanations? By the age of four, does she suggest to you how things might work? Are her explanations becoming increasingly complex? Are her explanations ingenious even if they are wrong?

★ Does she still watch and listen with interest when you show or tell her things?

# Questions and answers

It is natural for a small child to ask questions and to want to find out how things work. Children are born wanting to learn and gradually acquire the ability to pay attention, to think things through and to work things out.

## Just thinking!

Small children are naturally curious and thoughtful. To maintain that curiosity they need stimulation, encouragement to express their ideas and time to contemplate what has happened. A child's mind is like a library: the first task is to buy a book (to have the experience); the second is to decide which section to put it in (to contemplate what happened); and the third is to file and cross-reference (to compare what happened with other similar experiences). Remember this when you do things together. Activities are good in their own right, but the value of an activity for a child is talking about it or putting the treasures you found on display.

## What you can do

• Give your child a reason to gather information. For example, you could hunt for insects in the garden or collect all the snails.

• Encourage him to think about what he has gathered. For example, look at pictures of insects in books and find out their names, or talk about how snails move.

Encourage your child to gather information and think about what he has gathered.

# What the child learns

● To think first 'I can', and only when all else fails 'I can't'.

● To believe that thinking and working things out are fun.

● To voice an opinion and expect someone to listen. To expect an explanation. To feel good about themselves.

● To hold on to his natural curiosity and creativity beyond childhood. To look and listen for the unexpected.

● To become engrossed in an activity, which is the key to enjoyment.

● To 'fix' memories by putting them into words.

• Discuss how what he has learned can be extended to other things. What do butterflies and bees have that children do not (wings, more legs). Which other animals carry their houses about like snails?
• Make his life interesting. Cupboards bulging with toys are less important than activities, conversation, outings and quiet cuddles with you.
• Set a good example. Children learn by copying their parents. Go and take a look, listen, explore, be curious. Make 'I wonder why' your family motto.

## When I was as small as a pin...

Engage your child's imagination by encouraging him to speculate about how things could be different. For example, you could start by saying: 'When I was as small as a pin, I lived in a matchbox and I used to have rose petals for sheets. I could go swimming in soup bowls. I only needed five crumbs for my breakfast.' Then ask him to tell you what happened when he was as small as a pin.

**What you can do**
• Find a reason for a friendly argument. 'I don't like ice-cream.' 'Yes you do, I saw you eat it.' Keep it light and fun. Make silly statements that he can knock down.
• Ask why he thinks something happened. Protect his self-esteem by respecting his explanations even if they are wrong. Children who think they are stupid give up trying to be clever.
• Make your thoughts transparent. Tell him why you think it works that way. Explain simply, making sure he understands.
• Lively minds need lively conversation. Talk together, ask what he thinks will happen next, what is around the corner, or what he will do tomorrow.

## Listen and learn

Wherever you are, stimulate your child's interest in the world around him by encouraging him to use all his senses. Go out into the garden together at night and listen. Watch the birds coming in to roost and listen to their chirping. Listen to the sounds of waves on the beach, the wind in the trees, trains, or a quiet meadow on a summer's day.

**What you can do**
• Look out for things you might otherwise miss. How many red flowers can he see between here and the shops? How many green cars, or black cats? If he cannot count yet, do it for him – it is the looking that is important for the game.
• Look at your child when you speak to him. Small children find it easier to pay attention when they can see our faces.

## The way to the shops

Take a few photographs showing a route, for example from the house to the shops. Mount them in a scrapbook or on a strip of paper to make a wall frieze. Write 'To the shops' at the top and a few words about where each picture was taken underneath. Look at the photos in sequence with your child, discussing what they show and helping him to remember what you see on the way to the shops. Adults automatically organize thoughts into words, which makes it easy to remember and talk about experiences. Small children rely much more on memory pictures, which makes it more difficult for them. Your child will find it easiest to remember familiar outings, stories and books.

**What you can do**
• Talk with your child about the day's events. Use photographs to help him remember special occasions.
• Take familiar things, such as a few favourite toys, to help him remember the security of home when you are on holiday.
• Ask him to look for things you have lost.
• Play games that rely on his visual memory, such as picture lotto or the game in which you put all the cards face down on the table and turn them over two at a time to find a pair.

Looking at your child while you talk to them will encourage them to pay attention.

# That's funny!

One of the basic principles of learning is that if it makes you feel good you do it again, and if it makes you feel bad you avoid it if you can. It is easy for your child to feel clever when learning is pleasure. This is why laughter is good for reinforcing learning and instilling confidence.

## Put it into words and pictures

You can help your child remember the route from home to playschool if you make some silly landmarks along the way – for example, the bridge where you shout 'Howdy', the house with the barking dog, the shop with the glamorous clothes. She is too young to make maps of her world, but not too young to anticipate what will come next along a familiar route.

## What you can do

• Turn a sterile learning situation into a richer one with a little humour. It does not matter whether you count ordinary cats or cats in hats, you are still counting, but cats in hats are more fun.
• Devising silly images makes it easier for her to remember everyday things: her right hand is the one she uses to point to her nose; the letter S looks like a snake.
• Funny images can be strung together to make a special story for your child. Write it down. Children love their own personal stories, especially if they are funny.

Children find toilet humour very funny and revel in the rude.

## That's rude!

If there is a toilet in the doll's house, the people of the house will probably 'wee' more often than is strictly necessary. If the joke is about 'poo', she will tell it with more glee. As they sort out the acceptable from the unacceptable, children revel in the rude, the vulgar, the smutty and the downright sick. We can teach them nice rhymes that help them hear the little words of language, but they may learn to hear the little sounds more easily from the naughty rhymes their friends teach them.

Encouraging your child to laugh from an early age helps to develop their sense of humour.

## What you can do

• Have fun making a salt dough toilet for a doll's house.
• Be shocked! It is no fun for your child unless you are shocked by her rude joke.
• Read her stories about naughty animals and people.

## Tell me a joke

Laughing makes us feel good, and feeling good helps us to learn. To understand a joke, children need to be able to anticipate the predictable answer to a question and contrast it with the joke answer – a sophisticated process. She will tell jokes before she understands them. As she keeps on telling new jokes, she will gradually learn to understand why they are funny. Laughter probably makes the task easier for her to learn. The laughter of other children certainly makes practising the skill more enjoyable for her.

## What you can do

• 'Knock-knock' jokes and those that rely on word play ('What do you call a man with a spade in his head – Doug') are the easiest for children to understand.
• Encourage her joke-telling by laughing, whether or not the jokes are funny.
• Point out funny things in everyday life to help her develop a sense of humour.

## Tongue twisters

Learning to read and spell is a complex process and tongue twisters will not only make your child laugh, but they will also draw his attention to the little sounds that make up words.

## What you can do

• Repeat 'red lorry, yellow lorry' as fast as you can, ten times.
• Repeat the name Peggy Babcock ten times as fast as you can.
• Repeat the following tongue twisters:

Peter Piper picked a peck of pickled pepper;
A peck of pickled pepper Peter Piper picked;
If Peter Piper picked a peck of pickled
  pepper,
Where's the peck of pickled pepper Peter
  Piper picked?

Betty Botter bought some butter.
But she said the butter's bitter.
If I put it in my batter,
  it will make my batter bitter.
But a bit of better butter
  will make my batter better.
So she bought a bit of butter,
  better than her bitter butter,
  and she put it in her batter.
So 'twas better Betty Botter
  bought a bit of better butter.

# What the child learns

● That we approve of what she has done or said because we are laughing too.

● That a light-hearted attitude can be applied to the process of learning serious things.

● To have fun with siblings and friends.

● To make first moves into a wider social environment.

● A framework for logical thinking.

● Practice at holding two ideas in her mind at one time.

**Playing silly games together is fun for both of you.**

# Numbers, science and nature

The majority of young children have the fundamental skills of a good scientist: they are observant, curious and want to know why things happen. However, they are not true scientists yet. Until they are about seven years old, children cannot think logically – an essential scientific attribute.

## Thinking logically

Your young child does not weigh up all the evidence before jumping to conclusions. It is not simply that he cannot do so – under some conditions he can – but he does not do it reliably. Before the age of seven, he does not automatically classify things or reorganize information as adults do, so the things he has to remember are rarely stored in a way that he can access them.

It is rather like trying to find something in a disorganized room rather than in a neat filing cabinet. Disorganized thoughts are harder to keep in mind while he thinks of something else, and harder to remember when he tries to go back to them.

## How preschool children organize

Two-year-old children sort things into groups by comparing two items at a time. He puts a red shoe with a green shoe because they are both shoes, then adds a sweater with green stripes because it is green, and then a dress because it is striped.

By the age of three, he will be able to sort things by one attribute, such as colour, but not two attributes – size as well as colour. This 'one-dimensional' way of classifying things is quite rigid and does not allow for changing circumstances. For example, a five-year-old might say there is more water in a tall, thin glass than a short, fat one (even if they see you pour the water from one glass to another). In this one-dimensional classification, taller means bigger and the child ignores the width of the glass or the fact it is the same water in both glasses.

Help your toddler to order her thoughts by counting, sorting and matching.

## Sorting

For a young child, all the numbers above one are used to refer to a group of objects that have something in common – they are all buses or all flowers. Before a child can understand that numbers refer to groups of precise sizes, they have to understand the nature of groups, which is surprisingly difficult for very young children.

## Matching and sorting

Children often first learn to count by rote. However, in order for them to understand what one, two, three, four, five means, a child needs to be able to match each number with a precise quantity.

Matching one-to-one and sorting into groups are the skills that underpin the understanding of mathematics. Matching one-to-one is the process of pairing two quantities one-to-one. So you can match each cup with a saucer, each person with their clothes, each house with the person who lives in it. Sorting is putting things into groups. So the child can make a group of apples and a group of pears, or a group of twos and a group of fours.

## What you can do

- Listen when he explains.
- Explain carefully and simply when he asks.
- Read factual books to him.
- Encourage him to look carefully at his surroundings.
- Encourage matching and sorting activities.
- Concentrate on helping him to understand small numbers. For example, two is one for each hand. Three is one for him, one for Mummy and one for Daddy.

# Talent spotter

★ Even as a baby did he listen carefully and watch quietly? Does he still do so?

★ Does he often try to explain things, even if he gets the explanation wrong?

★ Do his explanations have their own simple logic? Are they getting increasingly complex as he gets older?

★ Is he especially interested in why things happen?

★ Does he enjoy building with construction kits more than playing with dolls (even macho ones)?

★ Is he fascinated by nature? Does he watch carefully and try to understand why things happen. Did you first notice this before he was three years old?

★ Can he name lots of flowers, makes of car, or breeds of dog, for example?

★ Does he enjoy factual books as much as, or more than, story books?

★ Does he use classifying words like 'red' or 'big' more often than other children of his age (see the Development Charts, pages 20–31)?

★ Is he often lost in thought? Is he more of a doer rather than a talker?

# Understanding numbers

Saying one, two, three does not mean a child understands numbers. She needs to know what four dogs and four cars have in common, and how four differs from three. This means she has to know how to sort things into groups and how to do simple addition so she can put numbers in order.

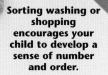

Sorting washing or shopping encourages your child to develop a sense of number and order.

## Sorting the socks

Collect all the odd socks you find in your drawers, and all the odd ones at the end of each wash. Put them in a box. The child's task is simple. She just tries to find all the pairs.

## What you can do

• Ask your child to help you put away the shopping. In this way she can practise sorting, for example by putting tins in one cupboard, biscuits in another.
• Similar activities include putting away the toys – puzzles on one shelf, dolls on another; and putting away her clothes – pants in one drawer, sweaters in another.
• Encourage your child to sort red bricks from green ones or large ones from small ones.

## A tiny Jamie donkey

To put things in order of size, she has to understand that each item must be compared with the others, that every comparison must be made on the basis of its size and that they must then be put in order. It is difficult and needs a lot of practice. One way to help her is to take a series she understands such as her family: big Daddy, little girl Georgia and baby brother Jamie. So Daddy has a big cake, Georgia a small cake and baby Jamie has a tiny cake; there is a big Daddy donkey, a small Georgia donkey and a tiny baby Jamie donkey.

## What you can do
• Young children tend to latch on to the extremes, such as the biggest and the smallest. At first, concentrate on bigger and smaller and forget about the ones in the middle. Later, introduce the idea of something very big, something very tiny and something in between.
• Talk about things being too big, too small and just right. Books and stories such as Goldilocks and the Three Bears can help.
• Look out for simple tray puzzles or pictures that show a series of ducks or cars, for example, arranged by size.

## One for each hand
In order to understand what the quantity 'two' means, a young child must match items one-to-one with a known reference. So, for example, the easiest way to understand the concept of two is to use her hands as a reference – one for each hand means two. To understand 'three', the easiest way may be to say one for me, one for you and one for Teddy.

## What to encourage
• Match one-to-one whenever the possibility arises. One sock for this foot and one sock for that foot, that is one foot, two feet – one sock, two socks.
• When she lays the table, she matches and sorts: one knife, one fork and one spoon for each person.
• One sweet for Mummy, one for Daddy and one for Frankie, that is three sweets.

Use getting dressed as an opportunity to practise counting.

• Start by just using one, two, three and four. Young children need to be able to see the quantity of objects at a glance if they are to make sense of what the names of the numbers mean and they can only do that up to three or four. Once she understands the principle that counting is matching a name with a specific quantity of objects or people, the principle can easily be extended to larger numbers.

## Board games

There is a variety of board games for young children. Some are based on the idea of matching one-to-one, others on simple counting – a piece is moved around squares on the board according to the roll of the dice.

### What you can do

• Select games in which the counters move in one direction only. Going from left to right and then from right to left (as in Snakes and Ladders) can be confusing.

# What the child learns

● The principle of forming groups, which underlies the principle of counting the items in each group.

● To understand that items can be arranged in order on the basis of a single characteristic.

● To understand that the words 'two' and 'three' refer to specific quantities.

● To match and sort – activities that underpin early mathematical understanding.

● To do something grown up and useful.

● To understand that counting is the principle of repeatedly adding one to the previous number.

• Games that depend on visual memory are much easier for her than they are for you; they are the most interesting ones to play with her.
• Avoid games based on strategy. Children under the age of seven find it impossible to weigh up alternative courses of action.

## Number plates

This is a simple game to play when you are out and about. It can be played in various ways depending on the age and knowledge of the child. At its simplest you look for numbers on number plates, but older children can start to do simple mental arithmetic playing this game.

### What you can do

• As you walk down the street, look at the number plates on cars and find different letters and numbers.
• Look for the numbers one to ten. Let each child 'bagsy' their age and see how many of this number they can find.
• Show younger children how to use their fingers to count and give them a number under ten to find. They can then count this number on their fingers.
• Get older children to add up the numbers on number plates. Can they find a number plate that adds up to ten?
• Encourage older children to spot words on the number plates, or make new ones by re-ordering the letters.

# Discovering science

Toddlers and preschool children may not be able to think logically or evaluate explanations, but they have all the other skills needed by great scientists: they are observant, curious and, above all, they want to know why.

## Nature table

The first stage in any scientific investigation is careful and systematic observation. Young children are not systematic, but they are very observant. Even if he does not have a long-term interest in nature study, setting up a nature table encourages careful observation.

### What you can do

• Look for insects by putting an old sheet under a bush and shaking the bush. You will be surprised how many insects you can collect. Put some of them into a jar with a few leaves from the bush and watch. Name those you can identify.
• If he shows an interest in finding out the names of different insects (or flowers or trees) get a reference book so that you can identify them together.
• Keep a diary of what he has seen to help him maintain his enthusiasm.
• Collect different flowers from the garden or different sorts of leaves. Classify and write the names on cards.
• Put a bird table in full view of the window. In winter, make bird cakes (see page 56) to encourage plenty of visitors.

Young children are naturally curious.

• Put slugs and snails on to the outside of the window (or on to a piece of clear perspex) and watch them slide along from underneath.
• Take bark rubbings by fixing a sheet of paper to the tree and, using a very soft pencil, scribble over a small area so you get an impression of the roughness and texture of the bark.

## Street games

Some children show no interest in wildlife. If your child is one of these, try classifying makes of cars or types of houses. Look for different road signs, types of manhole cover or garden gates – whatever takes his fancy. It may not be science, but these activities also require careful observation.

### What you can do

• Measure the street in strides. How many strides wide is each house? How many foot lengths per gate?
• Look at car number plates. How many can he see with a 3 on?
• Count the lampposts in the street.
• Ask where the water pipes, cables and phone lines run.

## Experiments

Young children are always experimenting. If you give your child a cup and a bowl of water, he will fill and pour, push the cup under the surface and watch the water rush in, and investigate why his sleeves get wet when he dips them in.

### What you can do

• Water and sand are the natural media for your child's experiments. Give him jugs to pour with, sieves that let through the dry grains of sand, and let him explore the difference between wet and dry sand. Why do some things such as sponges or sleeves soak up water, while others such as cups and raincoats let water flow into and over them? Why does water flow downhill? Encourage him to ask questions and pitch your explanations to his level.
• Show him something new – for example how a ping-pong ball jumps up to the

Encourage your child to experiment with natural objects.

surface if you release it under water, or how a toy boat will sink if you fill it up with water.
• If you do not remember any of the science you were taught at school, look out for science books designed for young children. They are often filled with simple and fascinating experiments and will also remind you of the explanations!

## Games with mirrors

Children can amuse themselves for hours experimenting with mirrors. Use a mirror with a backing – a hand mirror is ideal – or for the youngest children a metal mirror tile with the edges bound in tape.

# What the child learns

● Careful observation – an important building block for reading. The difference in the shape of words like 'dock' and 'clock', or 'bag' and 'beg' is in the fine detail.

● Encourages him to become involved. To concentrate, pay attention and to see things through from start to finish.

● To pay attention to small differences.

● To classify and group.

● Scientific 'experiments' teach him to think about the question 'why', to investigate questions for himself and to enjoy discovery.

Mirrors can be used for all sorts of games and experiments.

## What you can do

• Catch the sun in a small hand mirror and play the reflection on the wall.
• Put a dice or a small object in front of the mirror, then move it back. The dice in the mirror will move back by the same amount.
• Encourage her to look at her reflection in a still pool and see how the trees are reflected too. What happens when she throws a stone in the water?
• Write her name and hold it up to the mirror. What happens?
• Get her to try to put a chopstick into a mug by watching the reflection in the dressing table mirror. If that proves easy, put a plastic bottle in one hand and the chopstick in the other hand and try to get the chopstick into the neck of the bottle.
• If you have a dressing table with three mirrors, set it up to get multiple reflections. If not, buy three mirror tiles and use wide tape to make a line of three. Now let her look at her many reflections.
• If you have a wardrobe door with a mirror, stand her at the edge of the door and get her to lift her feet up – it looks as if both feet are off the ground!
• Get her to look at herself in the wardrobe mirror. What happens to the background if you move the door?

# Creativity with language

Between the bold swirls of her early drawings are the squiggles that become her writing. In her earliest pretend games are the actions and words of her first stories. Both aspects of language development need encouragement.

## The building blocks of creative writing

To form letters and words, we need skilled hands. To form sentences and tell stories, we need good language and organizational skills. To say things in a way that seems right or tell a story that grips the reader we need creativity. You may have a future author in the highchair but the mature fulfilment of her creative writing skills is a long way ahead. A child will not be creative in her use of language unless she hears it used creatively. She will look to you for guidance and is more likely to want to read and write if she sees you enjoying reading and writing.

## Tread carefully

Children learn by doing and do what they enjoy, before they understand that to write you must form letters and spell out words. In the preschool years, writing for fun and learning how to control a pencil is more important than forming letters and words correctly. Let your child's interest and skill dictate the pace.

The little squiggles in a child's early drawings will become her first writing.

## First writing

We often look for 'people' in the big swirls of her drawings, but tend to ignore the little squiggles. These, however, will become her first writing.

While you are writing your shopping list, give your child a pencil and a scrap of paper so she can make one too. This is an early attempt. A line of squiggles is bound to have something that looks like a letter. Tell her it is an N and show her an N on a label or in a book. Tread carefully. Praise her for writing with some letters like the ones in books, but do not overwhelm her with the entire alphabet.

## Beginning to write

With gentle encouragement she will soon be naming and forming most letters. Make sure you know how letters should be formed and, if she is ready, encourage her to join the dots you have made to form letters.

## What you can do

• Set a good example. If she never sees you writing, she will not write spontaneously. If she never sees you reading, she is unlikely to want to read early.
• Look out for the little squiggles in her drawings and talk about them with her.
• Encourage her to 'make lists' before you go shopping.
• Talk about the books and stories you have read together.
• Read poetry and stories which emphasize the rhyme and rhythm of language.
• Use words that express their meaning in their sounds, such as 'patter', 'roar', 'splash'.
• Introduce her to long words, such as competent, nocturnal, symmetrical.
• Play word games, especially silly ones she will enjoy.

# Talent spotter

★ Did she use words and actions to express herself before ten months? Was her language development precocious (see the Development Charts, pages 20–31)?

★ Is she able to express her feelings with unexpected maturity?

★ Does she play more elaborate pretend games than other children of the same age?

★ By the age of four, does she often talk to and for her toys? Does she tell her own story by organizing her toys into a little world she can control?

★ Does she 'write' without being asked directly?

★ Does she use words because she likes the way they sound to her?

★ By the age of four, does she enjoy telling stories? Are her stories becoming more elaborate as she grows older?

★ Is she often in a world of her own?

★ Does she become engrossed in the stories you tell her?

★ When you ask 'What did you do today?', is the answer purely factual or does she elaborate beyond the facts?

# Reading and writing activities

There is no need to rush to teach your child to read. By the age of ten, children in schools that start reading at seven are better readers than those that start reading at four. Instead, foster confidence, the skills that contribute to reading and a love of books.

Encourage your child to look for details in pictures.

## Practise 'seeing'

When children start to read they use pictures to guess what the word might be and then select the right one by its shape. With practice they learn to recognize shapes without the picture clues. This is also how adults read most of the time, except we often use the context of the sentence rather than pictures to make an initial guess. When we come across a new word we use a different method, sounding out the individual letters to make the word. This allows us to say the word even if we do not understand its meaning.

## What you can do

• Two-year-olds enjoy looking for details in pictures. Look for picture books that have a character who hides in each picture and ask him to find it. In the supermarket see if he can find his favourite cereal.
• Ask him to look for individual letters – perhaps the initial letter of his name – in books and on packaging.
• Look for words. Those that are repeated often such as 'the' are easiest to pick out.

# What the child learns

● That reading and writing are fun ways to communicate.

● That books provide a framework for the imagination.

● That shared stories are a way of getting and feeling close to someone else.

● That writing is a useful skill, for example to label what belongs to you or make a list of things to remember.

● That it is possible to become engrossed in stories.

---

• Label objects around the house so he learns to associate the word with the item.
• Help him develop an eye for detail. Play Hunt the Thimble, search for insects in the garden, do jigsaw puzzles. Encourage him to name flowers or the makes of cars to force him to look at the fine detail. Play games based on either matching or remembering pictures.
• Prepare your child for reading from left to right. The easiest way to teach this is to follow the words with your finger as you read to him; and it helps to lay out his clothes from left to right so the direction becomes natural.

## Practise sounding

To read new words, children must translate letters and groups of letters into sounds. So if you know what the sounds 'c', 't' and 'ar' make, you can put them together to make different words: art, arc, car, cart. To spell, children must do this in reverse. This is much harder, especially in English. A best guess usually gets the word (especially in context) but it is no help with spelling.

This is why spelling problems often persist. Those who help poor readers and spellers say that any activity that draws attention to the little sounds helps, and that the sooner parents start the better.

## What you can do

• Read nursery rhymes, poems and books written in rhyme to your child. Those who have problems reading usually have problems hearing the little sounds that make up words. Research suggests that practise in listening to the rhyme and rhythm can help them.
• Games such as I Spy encourage the child to listen to the little sounds.
• Play with rhymes and similar-sounding words when you talk to your child. Have fun by saying silly things such as 'Shall I put the queen's beans on your ghost toast or on the late plate'. He will soon pick up on the game and make up funny phrases of his own.

## Alphabet rhymes

Learning the alphabet is a lot harder than learning to count to ten because there are more letters and more opportunities to make mistakes. Your child needs a lot of practice.

### What you can do

• Here is a rhyme to help your child learn the alphabet:

**A** was an apple pie
**B** bit it
**C** cut it
**D** dealt it
**E** eats it
**F** fought for it
**G** got it
**H** had it
**I** inspected it
**J** jumped it
**K** kept it
**L** longed for it
**M** mourned for it
**N** nodded at it
**O** opened it
**P** prepared for it
**Q** questioned it
**R** ran for it
**S** stole it
**T** took it
**U** upset it
**V** viewed it
**W** wanted it
**XYZ** and ampersand
All wished for a piece in hand.

Give your child postcards to 'write' on.

## Learning to write

In order to write, a child must be able to use a pen with skill. The best practice is using a pencil or crayon skilfully. Tracing, copying, joining up dots and colouring in are all excellent practice for writing.

### What you can do

• Encourage him to 'write'. It may only be scribble but it will encourage him to think about writing and makes him feel important.
• If you give him small pieces of paper and a pencil, he is more likely to produce squiggles for himself.
• Write, make lists, take notes. He will want to do what you do.
• Stimulate hand–eye coordination. Dressing dolls, sewing, drawing – anything that requires fine hand movements will be of benefit.

# Story time

A child's first 'stories' are told in actions rather than words. She plays in her kitchen or feeds her teddy with a spoon. As she becomes more confident with language the stories become more complex and words play an increasing role.

## Telling stories

We often have difficulty in trying to describe an old friend we have not seen for a few years, although we would recognize them immediately if shown a photograph. Putting things – whether descriptions of events or people – into words can be hard, even if we are skilled with language.

Young children also lack the memory capacity to think about a whole story. They need props to help remind them what comes next. When your child is playing pretend games that mirror her life, the props help her to remember what comes next. She cooks in the kitchen, then she puts the pretend food on the plate. She moves the cows on her toy farm to the 'pond' for a drink. A young child's pretending games are her way of telling stories.

Provide your child with props to help her to act out a story.

## What you can do

• Provide your child with 'little world' toys, such as cars and road layouts or doll's houses, that give her practice in moving characters through a story. She can only tell stories if she knows the plot. Toys for pretence need to be rooted in her own experience. Give her the props she needs, such as dressing-up clothes, toy kitchens and toy cars. These will help her to act out a story in which she is the main character.

A child will get ideas for her own stories by listening to story tapes.

## Listening to stories

To listen effectively, young children need to look at us directly, which is why they often turn our faces so we are looking directly at them. So although they love videos, especially familiar ones, to truly appreciate stories they need books or storytellers. They only learn to love stories if listening is part of their daily life.

Bedtime stories, either read or invented by you are equally important. You might ask your child to suggest a theme or a character that you can incorporate into a story. Or you might consider using your child as a character in a fantastical adventure.

When you tell her a story you take on all the difficult bits, finding the words, remembering the plot, making it interesting. She just listens. If she enjoys your stories, in time she will want to tell stories too. Talk about the story as you tell it, or encourage her to interact with it – for example, by hiding from the spider or telling the naughty dog he is bad. This helps the child to tell her own stories when she is ready.

### What you can do

• For children today, stories come in many forms: books, tapes, videos and television. They all have their place. Videos and story tapes are great when you are busy, but do bear in mind that an active young child needs to play an active part in the story. Sometimes you need to be with them and to talk about the story.
• Read to them as often as you can.
• Interact with stories. Pat the rabbit, stroke the cat, pretend to be scared.
• Read favourite books again and again so she really gets to know the story.

• As she gets older, make sure she has access to plenty of story books, videos and story tapes to help her to move her games of pretence away from the domestic and into the wider world.
• Help your child to find the right props for retelling the 'story' of an unusual event, such as staying at a hotel or going out for a meal.

• Look out for things in everyday life that are similar to things she has seen in her stories – for example, a cat like the one in the book, houses like the one in the video, or cakes like the one the tiger liked. Reminding her of stories out of context encourages her to retell them to herself.

## Everyday stories

Talking together is always good for a child. A child who knows how to chat, to be funny and to express herself in an interesting way will always have plenty of friends. Find as many things to talk about as you can – the day's events, your plans for tomorrow, or what food she likes.

### What you can do

• Sit down with a drink and a bun and review the day. There is nothing like a good chat to boost story-telling ability.
• Talk about what you are going to do.
• Talk about what you have done.
• Look at family photos and talk about the occasions they record.
• Make plans and talk about them.
• Have silly conversations, use big words, read poetry and tell stories about your own world.
• The conversation around her is also part of her story. She may not know what 'work' is, but might know that it needs a tool bag or that people wear high heels and make-up there.

# What the child learns

● **How to tell a story and how, as she becomes more skilled, to make that story more complex.**

● **To listen and absorb information.**

● **To think about what has happened during the day and to tell that story to someone, even if at the moment she is only telling herself.**

Looking at photos of familiar events will encourage your child to talk about them.

# Following instructions

Even the most talented individuals need to take instruction – great tennis players employ coaches and great musicians have teachers. Talent – whether for sport or artistic expression – needs direction if it is to flourish, and this requires the ability to follow instructions.

Preschool children learn best by following your actions.

## At mother's knee

Two hundred years ago very few children had formal schooling. Girls learned the skills they needed at their mother's knee, boys at their father's side. At first they just watched; later they were shown how to do simple tasks. As they grew older, more was expected of them and they were shown how to do more complex tasks. Eventually they worked alongside their parents. This combination of watching, imitating and hands-on practice under the watchful eye of an expert is the ideal learning environment for young girls and boys.

## Working in stages

Children under the age of seven find it hard to remember instructions and carry out the task at the same time. It is easier for them to follow 'demonstrated' instructions step by step. Start by allowing your child to do the easier bits, while you take on those tasks that are likely to frustrate him. Guide him forward gradually and let him try. If he does not try for himself, how is he to know whether he could succeed.

## Developing skills

Practice makes perfect. Children are not born with practical skills, they develop them. Your child's talents need daily nurturing. Remember he is unlikely to want to do things you clearly hate doing. He will not want to knit if you make fun of those who knit. Bear this in mind and show enthusiasm for all the activities you want him to do. He does not need as much praise for activities that all the family love but he does need lots for those activities that some members of the family do not like.

## What you can do

• Select the right time for the activity. If he is being silly or restless, choose some other time.
• Let him see how much you enjoy doing things yourself.
• Let him see you do it. If he watches, he will have an idea what is required.
• Remove distractions. It is difficult for a child to follow instructions; he needs to give it his full attention.
• Look him in the face and tell him simply and clearly what has to be done.
• Break down tasks into short manageable parts that he can remember.
• Show him how. Words are much harder than actions for preschoolers to interpret and remember.
• Work alongside him.
• Nurture skills. Hands and eyes need practice. Show him again – it is hard to take it in first time around.
• Guide him step by step through the difficult bits.
• Praise effort not just results.
• Praise more than you correct.
• Make any criticism constructive.
• Show him you sometimes fail and that this is not a problem.

# Talent spotter

★ Does he listen and then try to do what is asked?

★ Does he need your praise or can he praise himself?

★ Is he able to accept criticism? Does he sulk if you try to correct him?

★ Is his hand–eye co-ordination good for his age so that he can carry out practical tasks without too much difficulty (see also the Development Charts, pages 20–31)?

★ Are his spatial abilities good? For example, is he good at seeing how to put things together so that he can complete puzzles and make things from construction kits?

★ Does he have the determination to persist at a task until he has succeeded?

★ Does he sit still and listen? Can he concentrate? Is he calm when things go wrong?

# Cooking and gardening

Teaching your child to help you in the kitchen and garden is a good way of giving practice in following instructions as well as introducing them to concepts such as weight and volume, and promoting interest in the natural world.

## Making a cake

Not all cooking is suitable for young children. A child is likely to forget your warnings, however often repeated, about hot fat or sharp knives. Dishes that your child can assemble and that you then cook in the oven are the best choices: cakes, stews, pizza, or baked pasta or rice dishes.

## What the child learns

● To follow simple instructions and work towards an end.

● To feel pride in what she can do. To take care of something. To be helpful and work with others.

● To use a measuring cup and/or scales.

● To sustain interest over a number of weeks.

● To observe and notice details.

## What you can do

• Cakes and tea breads are easy, especially those in which you carefully measure each ingredient and then mix everything together at once. She can do the measuring, the mixing, prepare the tins and put in the batter.
• Make a basic muffin batter. Your child can then add fresh fruit, chocolate or nuts and will enjoy greasing the tins and helping you spoon in the mixture.
• You need to work together to prepare a stew; you cut the meat and onions, she can deal with the softer vegetables. She can also help measure the liquid in a jug.
• Make or buy pizza bases and let her decorate them with ready-made tomato sauce, chopped cheese and other favourite toppings. Show her how to make funny faces on the pizza.

## Making a trifle

First cooking projects should be simple and allow a child to complete as much of the preparation as possible. However, it goes without saying that young children should not be left alone with sharp knives and hot pans or be allowed to put things into or take them out of the oven.

To make a trifle, only one ingredient, the custard, may need to be heated. If you use ready-made custard that does not need to be heated, your child can do everything herself. Otherwise prepare the custard for her and give it to her only when it has cooled.

Let her arrange pieces of cake in a bowl, pour in some sherry or fruit juice from a jug to moisten the cake, then spoon in some chopped fruit, and finally pour over the custard. Whip some cream until it is thick but not stiff. It is easier for her to deal with if it is still a little fluid. When the custard has set, let her spoon on the cream and then decorate the top of the trifle with a little grated chocolate or some coloured 'sprinkles'.

## What you can do

• For a party cake, melt some chocolate in an equal weight of cream. Cool and let her pour it over crushed digestive biscuits. Add a few nuts and either soaked and chopped prunes or chestnut purée. Put into a loaf tin and let it set in the refrigerator.

• Make small refrigerator cakes by mixing together melted cooking chocolate and butter. Add some cornflakes or another breakfast cereal and drop spoonfuls into individual paper cake cases.

• Cut up fruit for fruit salad.

• Make green salads or cut up cheese, cucumber and tomatoes for Greek salad.

• Make sandwiches.

• To make a simple ice cream, let her add sugar and flavourings (such as vanilla, mashed banana or strong black coffee) to

Cooking is a way of giving your child pride in a simple activity.

## Instant gardens

Most young children love to have a patch of garden to call their own. They like to see rapid results, so choose seeds that germinate quickly. Radishes and cress are the best choice. Sow them in batches so that there is always something happening. If this is still too slow, buy a few seedlings or potted plants, or transplant plants into her garden from somewhere else in yours. If you don't have access to a garden, make a mini garden in an old baking tin. Put in a good layer of compost. Collect moss to make a lawn, tiny flower heads for an instant flowerbed and arrange pebbles and shells for paths. She could even make a 'pond' with a small mirror. Water it carefully (it should not get soggy) and it will last a few days. You might consider growing a 'garden' in a window box if you lack access to the real thing.

### What you can do

• Cress will germinate on a plate of damp kitchen paper, cotton wool or an old wash cloth. Keep it moist.
• Radishes take six weeks from sowing to eating. Grow them in a tub on the patio or in a window box.
• Buy herb plants. They smell nice, have pretty flowers and because you only use a few leaves at a time they last a long time.
• Containers and grow-bags make ideal gardens for young children to grow potatoes, carrots, beans, tomatoes or salad vegetables.
• Children love things that grow taller than themselves. Try planting sunflowers, giant members of the onion family, tall grasses and reeds.

Pots are instant miniature gardens for your child to grow.

thick double cream. Freeze in an open tray until it is mushy (about 2–3 hours). Take it out, turn into a bowl and let her break up the ice crystals with a fork or a hand whisk. Put the ice cream back in the tray and freeze for another 2 hours.

# Just like you!

A child's enthusiasm for dusting the furniture or washing the kitchen floor can seem bizarre – but it is not drudgery if you can choose whether to do it. Simple domestic tasks provide invaluable learning opportunities and teach a child that people who care for each other do things for one another.

## Wash-day blues

Encourage your child to help you sort out the washing into different piles for different colours. This provides plenty of opportunity for practising sorting and, provided you keep an eye on him in case he puts your white sweater in the pile of red washing, there is very little that can go wrong.

## What you can do

• Let your child sort the dirty washing into white, light colours and dark colours, and divide large piles into loads.

• A young child can help you load the washing into the machine and help take it out. Let him hand you the pegs while you hang the washing on the line.

• Make piles of clean washing for each family member. He may not be able to fold all of the clothes, but he can put the socks in pairs.

• Let him practise hand-washing a few small items such as socks or doll's clothes. It needs organization to work through the stages of washing, rinsing and hanging up to dry.

Domestic tasks help children to develop a range of skills.

Encourage children to tidy up by making it a game.

## What you can do

• If everything has a 'home', he will be more systematic about how he tidies up and puts things away. He may also learn to imitate your organization.

• Keep bricks and puzzles in separate boxes and bags and then make sure that they are returned to the bag at the end of the game.

• Put one game away before getting out something new. As well as keeping things tidier, it will help him to concentrate on the current activity.

• If anything needs re-doing, wait until he has gone to bed so that he feels that he has been useful.

## Mopping the kitchen floor

By the time he starts school, he needs to know that tasks have a beginning, a middle and an end, and that once started they have to be completed. Mopping the floor is a good way to learn this because he can see where he has washed. Just show him the floor and give him the mop. You will need to squeeze it out for him at first.

## What you can do

• Housework provides lots of opportunities for questions. Why do sleeves get wet? Where does dust come from? Make sure you know the answers!

• Buy him a small mop and broom. These will be easier for him to use.

• Encourage and thank him when he has been helpful.

## Tidying up

For a small child tidying up is all part of the game; it is only later that he learns that it is a chore. If you start the tidying game early enough you may find it becomes a habit. Put on some music and see if he can pick everything up before the music stops.

## Copy cat

Whatever you do, he copies. Give your child plenty of practice in following instructions by playing copying games. Let him copy you as you pull funny faces, do silly walks or hop on one foot. You can also play verbal copying games. Ask him to respond to your questions by including the same words that you used:

*'Did you eat your breakfast?' – 'I did eat my breakfast.'*
*'Do you like sweets?' – 'I do like sweets.'*
*'Can I sit there?' – 'No!'*

You have caught him out. Saying the opposite is even harder.

### What you can do

• Play games like Simon Says in which he has to perform actions you suggest, provided you say the magic phrase 'Simon says'.
• Action rhymes and songs are excellent for copying movement.

Copying actions or words can be practised from an early age.

## What the child learns

● To be organized and systematic, and to plan.

● That if he takes out a toy he has to help put it away.

● To use his hands and his mind. To copy movements and to listen to instructions and follow them carefully.

● To be helpful and do things for other people.

● Manual dexterity, co-operation and organization.

● That everyone in the family helps in the house.

# Social skills

We can be just as creative in our interactions with other people as with painting, music, story-telling and scientific discovery. Indeed, this is one area of creativity where young children can excel.

## A significant achievement

Recent surveys suggest that 10–20 per cent of children do not have a friend, and a significant proportion of them will go through their school lives in this friendless state. Yet few of us list 'having friends' among our child's achievements!

## Competition or cooperation

The average preschool child is much more cooperative and helpful than an older child and is more cooperative than she will herself be when she gets older. Children model their social interactions on the people around them and, because most people are helpful and supportive to young children, children are usually helpful and supportive in return. Once they are exposed to the much more competitive world of school and playground, they usually become less helpful and more competitive. The more competitive the society, the less helpful are its children. If we want our children to remain cooperative, we have to make a concerted effort to set a good example in our social interactions.

Young children can often be surprisingly supportive and respectful of each other.

## Making friends

Children under the age of two do not form true friendships. They like to watch children their own age and to sit with them but they do not join in. They play in parallel rather than interacting in games together. Two-year-olds can return the friendship of others, but they do not know how to initiate friendship. So she can be friends with her older brothers and sisters and join in their games. Between the ages of two and three, they learn how to play with other children, but are usually attracted by the game a group of children are playing rather than the players.

From three onwards, children are more likely to choose to do what their friends are doing. Even at five or six, friendship may still be quite fleeting; her best friend today may be out of the picture by next month. At this age it becomes easier to pick out the popular children from the less popular. They start to exclude certain players and manipulate who joins the games. Once they are at school, children are less likely to be praised for being kind and helpful and this affects how children treat each other.

## What you can do

• Encourage her to be helpful. Let her help you clear up the toys, sort the washing or lay the table. Children who believe they should help each other, and see themselves within a culture that cares about people, are more likely to have better social skills.
• Set a good example by being polite and considerate within the family home.
• Reduce the level of competition. Give according to need. Do not try to give equally. Give uniquely.
• Expect and value respect and caring.

# Talent spotter

★ Even as a baby did she like to be in a crowd? When you first showed her books did she like the ones with people in them best?

★ When she is at nursery or playschool, does she choose who she wants to play with rather than an activity?

★ Do other children want to be her friend? When she arrives at nursery or playschool are other children pleased to see her?

★ Is she thoughtful, helpful and kind?

★ Does she have charm and does she use it? Is she persuasive?

★ Is she able to say what she wants and get what she wants without unpleasantness or aggression?

★ Is she upset by sad stories? Does she get upset when other children are hurt or upset?

★ Does she comfort you when you are feeling sad?

★ Does she laugh easily?

★ Is she less likely to sulk or lash out (physically or verbally) than other children of the same age?

★ Can she communicate well for age, see the Development Charts, pages 20–31)?

# Let's do it together

Children are born with a drive to be social. Long before they can talk, they will copy facial expressions and exchange smiles and gurgle in wordless conversations. Watching and being like us is how a young child learns the ways of the social world.

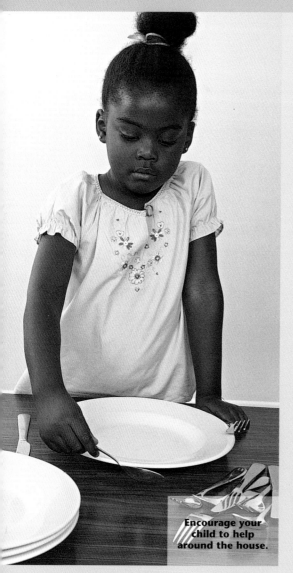

Encourage your child to help around the house.

## Helping

Children are natural mimics. The fact you are doing it is a major reason for him to give it a try. He would love to do the dishes, adores the dusting and would even clean the lavatory if you let him. He is not thinking about lightening your chores or giving you time to put your feet up; he is thinking about doing what you do. By the age of four and a half, he can take your feelings into account and if you show him that you appreciate his help, he is more likely to remain helpful. Make sure that you tell him that he is kind and helpful whenever he tries to be.

### What you can do

- Let him join in even if the job takes longer when he does so.
- Praise effort and do not let him see you redoing the job he helped you with. If he needs to do a bit extra, tell him. If you need to redo things, wait until he is in bed. He has to feel that you value what he does.
- Ask for his help and show your appreciation when it is given
- Expect him to appreciate what you do for him.

Counting games like Snakes and Ladders are fun for slightly older children.

# What the child learns

● The basic skills of sharing and caring. To think about others and to interact.

● To ask for and to give help. To feel and express sympathy.

● To play together without competing.

● To have fun if they lose. That playing together is fun.

● That even mistakes can be shared.

• Explain that friends and families support each other and do things for each other and that people are more likely to want him to be their friend if he is kind and helpful towards them.

## Scissors, Paper, Stone

Societies in which people are more cooperative tend to play games of chance; those that are more competitive and dictatorial are more likely to play competitive games. Originally a Japanese betting game, Scissors, Paper, Stone was brought back to the West by sailors. It is a great way to fill a spare ten minutes. It can be slow for a youngster or fast and furious for older children. Play it in pairs. Each child sometimes loses and sometimes wins. But they play it so many times that they lose count. Each person puts one hand behind their back and makes one of the following shapes: scissors, with the fingers snipping; paper, with a flat hand; stone, with the hand in a fist. On the count of three each child shows their hand. Scissors beats paper (because it can cut), paper beats stone (because it can wrap it), stone beats scissors (because it can blunt them).

### What you can do

• Play board games like snakes and ladders, where the winner and loser are determined by a throw of the dice rather than skilful play.
• Choose games where the only competition is with themselves, such as throwing balls into buckets.
• Try and encourage your child to realise that the fun is in the playing and not necessarily in the winning, and that understanding simple rules and playing together with other children is an enjoyable activity in itself.

Some old-fashioned games can be magical for children to play.

## Chinese Whispers

This is an old party favourite and probably only suitable for children over the age of five. You whisper something to the first child; he says what he has heard to the second, and so on down the line. If there are a lot of children, get two or three messages going in different directions. The whole point of the game is to get it wrong and laugh at the end result.

**What you can do**

• Play as many non-competitive games as possible. Traditional circle games like Ring-o-Roses are obvious choices. Even Pass the Parcel can be made less competitive by putting a little present between each layer.

## Tin-can telephone

This game may be old-fashioned, but it encourages children to be sociable and to talk to each other.

**What you can do**

• You need two tins. As these are going to be put against the child's ear they should not have sharp edges. Cocoa tins are ideal but snack containers work too. You also need a long length of string.

• Make a hole in the bottom of each can with a skewer (for metal and card) or with a hot metal knitting needle (for plastic). Parents should do this for younger children and must supervise older children. Poke one end of the string through the hole in the can and tie a big knot inside the can. You may need to tie the knot to be sure it does not slip through the hole when the string is pulled tight. Do the same with the other can and the other end of the string.

• To play, one child whispers into her can and the other child puts his can to his ear to listen. This only works if the string is kept very tight and this will inevitably lead to the string being pulled out from the can, but it can easily be put back.

# Just friends

Friendship needs practice. Although you can help by teaching her to be kind and how to cope with losing, sooner or later she needs direct experience of the give and take of friendship.

## Pets

A young child cannot take sole responsibility for a pet, but she can help look after one. The older the child, the more responsibility you can hand over, but you will have to remain in the background to ensure the pet does not come to any harm. Caring for a pet teaches a child sympathy and empathy and also gives them a topic of conversation when friends visit.

### What you can do

• A pet plant is probably the best starting place. It is much less traumatic if it dies. Set her the task of looking after one for a few weeks as a precondition for getting a pet.

• Insects can be collected in a jam jar along with some leaves and kept as pets for a day and then put back in the garden.

• Goldfish are easy but rather dull and birds can be difficult for a small child to handle. The best first pet for a young child is probably a hamster. Hamsters have the advantage over gerbils and rats in that they are solitary animals, so keeping just one is not cruel. They do not smell as much as mice and their cages need cleaning less often than those of guinea pigs or rabbits.

A guinea pig is an ideal first pet for a child.

Games with clearly defined roles can prevent jealousy and over-possessiveness about toys.

## Let's play

It is sometimes hard for two children who do not know each other to play together. Three-year-olds can be very possessive about their toys, however much they promise to share before their friend arrives. The easiest way to cope is to set up an activity both children can share and where rules or roles are clearly defined, such as playing shops.

### What you can do

• Before a child comes round to play, let your child choose which toys you will get out and which are to stay in the cupboard. Toys are her most important possessions. She may not want to share them any more than you might want to share your new car with a friend.
• Encourage the children to swap roles halfway through a game so that everyone has the chance to use all of the props.
• Involve both children in choosing and making the props – for example, cutting out cardboard fish for a fish shop.

• Be prepared to mediate if the children have a disagreement. It may be wise to prepare for a quiet play activity like drawing if they seem to be becoming irritable or overexcited.

## Songs with actions

Young children may need your help to break the ice when they first meet. Playing a singing game with actions can be a good way to get them laughing together. Sing:

*Head and shoulders, knees and toes, knees and toes,*
*Head and shoulders, knees and toes, knees and toes,*
*And eyes and ears and mouth and nose*
*Head and shoulders, knees and toes, knees and toes.*

Touch each part of the body as it is mentioned in the song. The second time you sing you do not say 'toes' but still carry out the action. Next time omit the

# What the child learns

● To have empathy and sympathy for other creatures.

● To care for something on a day-to-day basis.

● To share his possessions with good grace and generosity.

● To enjoy playing with other children.

● To respect other people's needs and wishes.

word 'knees', and so on until you are not mentioning any parts of the body at all – just doing the actions.

**What you can do**
• Get a book or tape if you need inspiration for more action songs, or ask a teacher at the nursery.
• Make up your own actions to a song you already know. Two famous examples are given here:

I'm a little teapot
*I'm a little teapot short and stout*
Action: One hand on hip

*Here's my handle, here's my spout*
Action: One arm makes a spout

*When the kettle's boiling hear me shout*
*Pick me up and pour me out.*
Action: Bend from the waist in a pouring movement

Singing action songs helps to break the ice when children first meet.

# Index

# Acknowledgements

Executive Editor **Jane McIntosh**
Editor **Kate Tuckett**
Design Manager **Tokiko Morishima**
Designer **Peter Gerrish**
Production Conroller **Ian Paton**

Picture credits

**Octopus Publishing Group Limited/Adrian Pope** 1 bottom right, 2 bottom right, 2 bottom left,
3 bottom left, 7 top centre, 8 bottom left, 9 top right, 15 top right, 75 centre bottom, 87 top,
89 centre right, 90 top left, 91 top right, 108 bottom left, 112 bottom, 115 top right, 116 top right,
116 top left, 124 top, 125 bottom, 126 bottom right, 129, 134 bottom, 136 bottom left, 138 top right,
139 centre right, 141, 149 right centre top, 152 bottom left.
**Peter Pugh-Cook** 3 bottom right, 4 centre bottom, 11 top right, 13 bottom left, 17 bottom right,
19 bottom left, 32 top left, 32 top right above, 33 bottom centre, 37 top, 38 top left, 39 bottom right,
40 top left, 41 top right, 42 bottom left, 45 top left, 45 bottom left, 46 top left, 47 centre right,
48 bottom left, 48 top left, 50 bottom, 53 top, 54 centre left, 55 centre right, 58 centre right,
61 top right, 61 bottom right, 62 insert top right, 62 top, 63 bottom right, 64 top left, 65 top right,
66 top left, 66 bottom left, 68 bottom left, 69 top right, 70 top, 71 centre right, 72 top, 73 top right,
74 top left, 74 top right, 76 bottom left, 77 bottom right, 78 bottom left, 79 top right, 80 top left,
81 centre right, 82 centre right, 83 bottom right, 84 bottom left, 88 top left, 92 bottom left,
93 bottom right, 94 centre left, 95 top right, 96 top left, 97 bottom right, 98 top left, 99 bottom left,
100 bottom centre, 103 top right, 104 bottom left, 105 centre right, 106 bottom left, 107 top right,
110 bottom left, 113 bottom right, 114 bottom left, 117 bottom, 118 bottom left, 120 bottom left,
122 bottom left, 123 centre right, 128 bottom left, 131 centre right, 132 top right, 133 top right,
140 centre left, 142 bottom left, 145 bottom centre, 146 top left, 147 centre right, 148 top left,
150 bottom, 153 top left, 154 top, 155 centre right, 156 top, 157 top right, 57 bottom left